D1409499

DIVORCE AND REMARRIAGE
What Does the Bible *Really* Say?

Ralph Edward Woodrow

International Standard Book Number: 0-916938-06-9
Library of Congress Catalog Card Number: 82-99960
©1982 by Ralph Woodrow Evangelistic Association, Inc.
Printed in the United States of America

Additional copies of this book may be obtained through your local bookstore or Ralph Woodrow, Post Office Box 124, Riverside, CA. 92502. Single copies: ▓▓▓. Quantity prices on request.

CONTENTS

1. God Hates Divorce?..................................... 5

2. Divorce For Every Cause?....................... 15

3. Except It Be For Fornication.................. 29

4. Forbidding To Marry............................. 45

5. Questions From Corinthian Converts........ 57

6. Living in Adultery?................................. 73

7. Straining At a Gnat............................... 95

Notes.. 111

1

GOD HATES DIVORCE?

"I know the Bible speaks against divorce all the way from Genesis to Revelation!" These were the words of a young man by the name of Andy as he talked with his pastor. But Andy—

"Nevertheless what saith the scripture?" (Gal. 4:30).

like many people—was in error on this point. Over the years he had heard sermons against the evils of divorce, but he had never really studied the matter out *in his own Bible!*

Does the Bible condemn *all* cases of divorce and remarriage? No, it does not. Turning to Deuteronomy 24:1-3, we read:

"When a man hath taken a wife, and married her, and it come to pass that she find no favor in his eyes, because he hath found some uncleanness in her: then let him write her a bill of divorcement, and give it in her hand, and send her out of his house. And when she is departed out of his house, *she may go and be another man's wife.*"

Divorce, though not directly instituted by God, is nevertheless accepted and recognized in the Bible as a fact of human life. When Moses required the "bill of divorcement," he only sought to give the practice a *legal* basis. The custom itself had been around a long time before Moses (cf. Gen. 21:10-14). *The Interpreter's Bible* has well said: "There is no law in the Old Testament which institutes [divorce] because it is simply taken for granted as part of age-old custom. What the law tries to do is regulate it."[1]

Instead of divorce *never* being allowed under the law of Moses, there were only *two* situations mentioned in which a man could *not* divorce his wife! (1) If he accused her of premarital intercourse and she was proven innocent, he could never put her away (Deut. 22:13-19), or (2) If he forced a virgin (who was not engaged) into a sexual relationship, he was to marry her and never put her away (Deut. 22:28, 29). Otherwise, divorce was permitted and practiced. Had divorce been forbidden in *all* cases — as some have assumed — the *penalty* in these two passages would be meaningless.

Was God against divorce all the way from Genesis to Revelation in the Bible? Well, let's see.

In *Genesis,* God instituted marriage at the beginning. At that point the idea of divorce and remarriage was obviously absent. It would have been *impossible* — there were no other people in the garden of Eden! Adam and Eve became "one" in marriage and this — not divorce — was the *ideal.* However, before we leave Genesis to continue our study on through the books of the Bible, we find Abraham — *"faithful* Abraham" (Gal. 3:9) — involved in divorce! What seems especially significant to our present study is that he put Hagar away — not in *disobedience* to God — but in *obedience* to what God told him to do! He was told to obey the words which are now scripture, "Cast out this bond woman" (Gen. 21:10-14; Gal. 4:30). There is nothing against divorce, as such, in Genesis.

In *Exodus,* if a man took a slave girl he had purchased for a wife, and later decided to put her away, he was not to *sell* her, "seeing he hath dealt deceitfully with her." And, "if he take him another wife; her food, her raiment, and her duty of marriage, shall he not diminish. If he do not these three unto her, then she shall go out free" (Exodus 21:7-11). If he neglected her in any one of these three areas, she was no longer

6

obligated to stay with him. The basis of putting away was thus regulated by the law, but the practice itself was taken for granted. She was free from that marriage just like a released slave was free from slavery. Though Exodus is loaded with rules and regulations about many things, it says nothing against divorce.

In *Leviticus,* a priest was not to marry a "divorced" woman, but neither was he to marry a widow (Lev. 21:7, 14). Such regulations — among *many* regulations mentioned — applied only to *priests.* It was no sin for men who were not priests to marry divorced women. The practice was common and unquestioned.

In *Numbers,* divorced women are again mentioned right along with widows — not as sinful women — but in a passage dealing with vows (Numbers 30:9).

In *Deuteronomy,* a man who put away his wife was to "let her go whither she will" and was not to "sell her at all for money" (Deut. 21:13, 14). A divorced woman was free to "go and be another man's wife" (Deut. 24:2). There is nothing against divorce in Deuteronomy.

Believe it or not, as one continues on through the books of the Old Testament, there is *not one verse* against divorce until the very last book — Malachi — and that verse has been commonly *misunderstood!*

MALACHI 2:16

"For the Lord, the God of Israel, saith that he hateth putting away" or, as it is commonly summarized, God hates divorce. This verse is often quoted by those who suppose all divorce is sinful, but they fail to show *what kind* of divorce was meant!

There is no disagreement that marriage was the original ideal — not divorce. But to say that God *never* approves of

7

divorce, that he hates *all* divorce — and to quote this verse as a proof text — is unscholarly and inexcusable. *God himself* is represented as putting away his wife Israel and giving her a bill of divorce (Jer. 3:8). If *all* divorce was hated by God, if *all* divorce was sinful, then God himself committed sin and did that which he hated! This is absurd.

It can easily be seen within the Bible that God not only permitted divorce, in some situations he actually commanded it! At one time "many" of the Jews — including priests, religious singers, and others — had married foreign wives. Children had been born into some of these marriages. Yet in a time of repentance — with prayer, weeping, and trembling — they were told to do God's pleasure and put away these wives! It is all spelled out in detail in Ezra 10.

If the meaning in Malachi 2:16 was that *all* cases of divorce were "hated" by God, how can we explain that divorce was his "pleasure" in Ezra 10:11? Obviously each passage must be understood *within its proper setting.*

In the Ezra passage, Jewish men had married foreign wives, contrary to the law that said: "Neither shalt thou make marriages with them [foreigners who worshipped other gods]: thy daughter thou shalt not give unto his son, nor his daughter shalt thou take unto thy son. *For* they will turn away thy son from following me, that they may serve *other gods"* (Deut. 7:14). The issue was not just racial, it was *religious.*

In the Malachi passage, a similar situation existed in that Jewish men had contracted marriages with foreign women — and forsook their wives for the purpose of doing this! People who belong to the heavenly Father are called the "sons and daughters" of the true God (2 Cor. 6:18). But — in contrast to these — the women these men married were *daughters of a strange god!* "Judah hath dealt treacherously, and an abomination is committed in Israel...Judah hath married the daughter of a strange god" (Mal. 2:11). Men were forsaking their wives

8

for young, foreign women who worshipped other gods! It was *this kind* of divorce that God hated. Taking the verse in context qualifies the whole thing.

To quote this one verse as though *all* cases of divorce were hateful to God is very unsound. One might just as logically quote Deuteronomy 7:1-4 and say God hated *marriage!* The passage in Deuteronomy was against marriage because of the *kind* of marriage it was — marriage to foreign women who worshipped heathen gods. The passage in Malachi spoke against divorce because of the *kind* of divorce it was — men were casting aside their wives in order to marry foreign women who worshipped heathen gods. We must not take this text out of its context and conclude that *all* divorce is sinful, for (as we have seen), divorce was not only permitted in the Bible, in some circumstances it was commanded, and even God himself put away Israel, his unfaithful wife!

A VARIANT READING

But there is another side of the coin concerning Malachi 2:16 that has commonly been overlooked. *"If* the text is correct," says the scholarly commentary known as *The Interpreter's Bible,* it is an idea "which is found *nowhere* else in the Old Testament — that God is opposed to divorce."[2] "If" the text is correct? Is there some question about this particular verse? Yes, there is. This happens to be a verse for which there is a variant reading in the oldest manuscripts. In that place where the King James text says, "For the Lord, the God of Israel, saith that he hateth putting away," the King James margin (which gives the variant reading) says, "For the Lord, the God of Israel, saith if he hate her, *put her away"*!

Needless to say, this puts a different slant on the whole thing! This is also the reading of the Latin Vulgate which served as the basis for the translation of the Douay (Roman Catholic) version: "When thou shalt hate her put her away, saith the

9

Lord the God of Israel." Since the Roman Catholic church is noted for its opposition to divorce, this wording would have been used only because the translators believed it had the strongest authority. The Targum (in agreement with the Septuagint version which the apostles *often* quoted from in the New Testament) says in its paraphrase, "If thou hate her, divorce her."

According to Josephus, under Jewish law a woman "could not of herself be married to another, unless her husband put her away." Apparently what had become a common practice at the time of Malachi was that a man would merely cast aside his wife, as Matthew Henry said, "without the ceremony that the law of Moses prescribed." He would cast her out without granting a bill of divorce, for she was still referred to as his "companion, and the wife of his covenant" (Mal. 2:14). So, this verse was saying that if a man hated his wife, he should at least put her away legally. She could then go "and become another man's wife," hopefully finding a man who would love her and be true to her.

There are 23,214 verses within the Old Testament. Isn't it strange that those who suppose God hates *all* divorce, that *all* divorce is sinful, must go through 23,188 verses — clear over to Malachi 2:16 (with only 26 verses remaining) — in order to find *one verse* against divorce! They quote this verse as though it was the very theme of the Bible. They fail to take the context of this one verse into consideration. They form dogmatic conclusions on wording for which there is a strong variant reading in the oldest manuscripts and which, if correct, is the very opposite of the point they try to make!

ONLY DEATH CAN SEVER?

After quoting this one verse in Malachi, those who would have people believe the Bible is against divorce "all the way from Genesis to Revelation," then rush over to Romans 7:1-4

10

to reinforce their claim that only *death* — not divorce — can sever the marriage bond.

> "Know ye not, brethren, (for I speak to them that know the law,) how that the *law* hath dominion over a man as long as he liveth? For the woman which hath an husband is bound by the law to her husband *so long as he liveth;* but if the husband be *dead,* she is loosed from the law of her husband. So then if, while her husband liveth, she be married to another man, she shall be called an *adulteress:* but if her husband be dead, she is free from that law; so that she is no adulteress, though she be married to another man. Wherefore...."

We must bear in mind that Paul's illustration here was from the law. If the whole policy regarding divorce and remarriage was changed in the New Testament — as some suppose — this could not be the point here. Paul is referring back to the *law.* That his statement was only *general* in nature (without going into all details) is evident, for under the law a woman was *not* bound to her husband *if he divorced her.* In that case she *could* remarry and was *not* called an "adulteress" while her former husband lived! She *could* "go and be another man's wife" — a *wife,* not an adulteress (Deut. 24:1-4). Paul did not say, "A woman who is divorced is still bound to her husband as long as he liveth," for such was obviously not the case.

"The law was given by Moses"
(John 1:17).

Another exception under the "law" was this: a woman was not bound to her husband if, because of polygamy, he neglected her in certain ways. She was allowed to go free (Exodus 21:11). Paul knew these things — obviously — and those to whom he wrote "who knew the law" did also. But in making his basic point, *he simply did not go into details that were not essential to that point.*

If the reader will take time to get the flow of thought in the context of Romans 7:1-4, the *general* nature of Paul's statement will be evident. To put it briefly, Paul gave various contrasts between the old life of sin and the new life in Christ. We were once bound to the law, condemned by the law in sin. But we have been crucified with Christ, we died — spiritually speaking — and since the law only has dominion over a person as long as he lives, we are now free to "be married to another, even to him who is raised from the dead, that we should bring forth fruit unto God" (verse 4). This is the point Paul sought to make and for which he gave the illustration about a woman being bound by the law to her husband until death.

GENERAL STATEMENTS

Language permits the use of general statements such as this without branching out to all explanations or exceptions that might be possible. Many examples of this could be given, but it is so self-evident, the following Biblical example will suffice.

In contrast to the *repeated* sacrifices of the Old Testament, the apostle says Christ *"once*...appeared to put away sin by the sacrifice of himself. And as it is appointed unto men *once* to die...*So* Christ was *once* offered to bear the sins of many" (Heb. 9:26-28). The emphasis is on the word "once" in this familiar passage. Christ appeared *once* to put away sin. To illustrate this, the apostle says it is like the fact that it is appointed unto men *once* to die. In using this example, he does not digress from his over-all point by explaining exceptions. But there were exceptions! *All* men did not die only once, for people in the Bible who were raised from the dead and later

12

died, died *two* times! And, according to Paul, there will be others who will not even die *one* time—if alive at the coming of Christ! (1 Cor. 15:51; 1 Thess. 4:16, 17). But to have included all of this information in Hebrews 9:27 would have only clouded the general point that was being made.

This same principle applies to Paul's statement to the Corinthians: "The wife is bound by the law as long as her husband liveth; but if her husband be dead, she is at liberty to be married to whom she will; only in the Lord" (1 Cor. 7:39). This concept—that a woman whose husband was dead was allowed to marry—was a basic law among all countries. If she was divorced, she was also free to marry again in certain circumstances, but Paul was not dealing with this.

It is understandable that some of the Corinthian converts, having come from a background of gross immorality (1 Cor. 6:11), might swing to the other extreme—questioning all sexual contact, even in marriage. In questions they had written to Paul, they had asked if it was better for a person to be single, if a believer should leave an unbeliever, if a virgin should marry, and—apparently—even questioned whether a woman should remarry whose husband was *dead*. Adam Clarke says that Paul's statement "seems to be spoken in answer to some question of the Corinthians to this effect: 'May a woman remarry whose husband is dead?'... To which he replies, in general, that... if the husband die, she is free to remarry, but only in the Lord."[3]

Paul cited a general principle of the law in agreement with his teaching. Again, as in Romans 7:14, we must bear in mind that the purpose of Paul's brief reference to the law was to state a general principle only. To have included wording about possible exceptions would have detracted from the point he was making.

When God put away his wife Israel, she was given a bill of divorce (Jer. 3:1, 8). By this action, she was no longer bound to him (cf. Deut. 24:1-4). Now, if the *only* way a woman could be released from the marriage bond was through her husband's death — as some try to read into Romans 7:1-4 and 1 Corinthians 7:39 — then Israel's release would have required the *death of God*. It is ridiculous. If only death can dissolve marriage, we must ask: *When did God die?*

JOHN THE BAPTIST AND HEROD

Some have supposed Old Testament law was against divorce because of the words of John the Baptist to Herod, but this is not the case. Herod had put John "in prison for Herodias' sake, his brother Philip's wife: for he had married her. For John had said unto Herod, It is not *lawful* for thee to have *thy brother's wife*" (Mark 6:17, 18; Matt. 14:3, 4). John was not saying that divorce and remarriage were not lawful. Under the law, if a woman had been granted a bill of divorce, she was free to become another man's wife. The reason Herod's actions were not "lawful" was because marriage to a brother's wife was considered *incest* (Lev. 18:16). Clearly, this was the point that John made: "It is not lawful for thee to have *thy brother's wife.*"

In the study of Biblical doctrines — including the subject of divorce and remarriage — it is important that we seek to understand statements as they were originally intended. Everything should be understood within its proper setting and context.

14

2

DIVORCE FOR EVERY CAUSE?

At the time of Jesus, a type of divorce known as divorce "for every cause" had become quite popular among some of the Jewish people. It was a controversial issue and by asking if this type of divorce was lawful, the Pharisees attempted to put Jesus on the spot. Thus we read:

"The Pharisees came...tempting him, and saying..." (Matt. 19:3).

"The Pharisees also came unto him, *tempting* him, and saying unto him, Is it lawful for a man to put away his wife *for every cause?* And he answered and said unto them, Have ye not read, that he which made them at the beginning made them male and female, and said, For this cause shall a man leave father and mother, and shall cleave to his wife: and they twain shall be one flesh?...What therefore God hath joined together, let not man put asunder.

"They say unto him, Why did Moses then command to give a writing of divorcement, and to put her away? He saith unto them, Moses because of the hardness of your hearts suffered you to put away your wives: but from the beginning it was not so.

"And I say unto you, Whosoever shall put away his wife, *except it be for fornication,* and shall marry another, committeth adultery: and whoso marrieth her which is put away doth commit adultery.

"His diciples say unto him, If the case of the man be so with his wife, it is not good to marry. But he said unto them, *All men cannot receive this saying,* save they to whom it is given" (Matt. 19:3-11; see also Mark 10:2-12).

The question of the **Pharisees,** "It is lawful for a man to put away his wife for every cause?" was asked for the purpose of "tempting" Jesus. It was a trick question about a subject on which the Jewish people were sharply divided. Divorce "for every cause" was taught by Rabbi Hillel and had become very popular at the time — even minor offenses of a man's wife were included as causes for divorce. This teaching was in contrast to that of Rabbi Shammai who limited divorce to major offenses of misconduct or immorality.

Much of this dispute centered on the interpretation of the word "uncleanness' in Deuteronomy 24:1, 2:

> "When a man hath taken a wife...and it come to pass that she find no favor in his eyes, because he hath found some *uncleanness* in her: then let him write her a bill of divorcement...and when she is departed out of his house, she may go and be another man's wife."

Under the law, a woman could be stoned to death for offenses such as adultery or even premarital sin (Lev. 20:10; Deut. 22:21). In such cases, a man would not need a divorce in order to remarry! Consequently, this "uncleanness" had been applied to many lesser evils by the school of Rabbi Hillel. It had developed into the practice of divorce "for every cause"; that is, almost any cause was used as an excuse.

Josephus, the first century Jewish historian, put it like this: "He that desires to be divorced from his wife *for any cause whatsoever* (and *many* such causes happen among men,) let him in writing give assurance that he will never use her as his wife anymore, for by these means she may be at liberty to marry another husband."[4] Josephus himself had divorced two wives for comparitively trivial reasons.

"Causes" for divorce at the time of Jesus ranged from cases of barreness to such things as serving food on which the tithe had not been paid, appearing in public with disheaveled hair, being a poor housekeeper, having a bad reputation, not seasoning the soup right, burning the biscuits, and even if the man simply found a woman he liked better![5]

When a man found a woman he "liked better," he would find some excuse to put his wife away and that for *the express purpose of marrying this other woman*. So it is understood by Charles B. Williams in his translation, citing an Aramaic source as expressing *purpose:* "...who divorces his wife *to* marry another woman."[6] It is plain to see that divorce on this basis was not the same as divorce when there were valid grounds.

With women being put away for any cause, marriage vows had little meaning. The woman at Jacob's well who had had five husbands was probably a victim of this abuse (John 4:18). Even the Jewish *Talmud* says the water of jealousy test for adultery (see Numbers 5) lasped into disuse by this time — adultery being so common that God no longer inflicted the curses. Jesus referred to it as an *"adulterous* generation" (Matt. 12:39).

Jewish men who put away their wives for any cause were highly inconsistent. They might be ready to condemn to death a woman taken in adultery (John 8:4-6), yet their practices were really no better. Though they went through the formality of a "divorce" and contracted another "marriage," such marriages were little more than *temporary* arrangements. Some were *very* temporary. Edersheim cites two instances of rabbis who proclaimed their wish to be married *for a day,* and then divorce, in exercise of their rights![7] With a blunt, sweeping statement, Jesus branded this whole practice of divorce for any cause just exactly what it amounted to: *adultery*. It was *this kind* of divorce that Jesus condemned.

Some assume that Jesus condemned *all* kinds of divorce and *all* cases of divorce. This can hardly be the case, for the discussion was about what was "lawful," and there is not one verse in the law that condemned divorce when there was a real cause.

Even God himself is represented as putting away his wife Israel. We should not assume that he who came "to destroy not the law...but to fulfill" (Matt. 5:17), was teaching that the Old Testament law which permitted divorce was wrong. He spoke not against the law itself, but against *the abuse of that law.*

A GENERAL STATEMENT

If we will follow the same sound, recognized rules of interpretation that we would on other Biblical subjects, we can find strong reasons to believe that what Jesus said against divorce and remarriage was a *general* statement. As such, his statement could condemn divorce "for any cause"—when used as an excuse—and yet not condemn *all* cases of divorce. If there was a valid reason, such as "fornication," this was clearly a different matter. This *exception* is mentioned right within the divorce passage (Matt. 19:9).

Even though the saying of Jesus includes the word "whosoever," this was simply a manner of speaking which cannot mean all without exception. The very wording "whosoever...*except"* shows this. It is like the word "all" which is often qualified by the context. When "all" Judah went out to hear John, when "all" were baptized by him, when "all" wondered if he was the Christ (Mark 1:5; Luke 3:15), "all" included a wide range of people, different classes and kinds of people, but not all people *absolutely.* Terms such as "all" or "whosoever" can mean all without certain distinctions and yet not all without exception. Such is clearly the case here.

Anyhow, in the saying of Jesus against the "every cause" type of divorce, we need not suppose ALL divorce was condemned. If one will take the time to carefully, and prayerfully, look at this entire passage (Matt. 19:3-11), it becomes evident that we are looking at *a whole series of general statements*—statements that were never intended to explain *all* details about *all* cases.

18

ALL COUPLES JOINED BY GOD?

When Jesus said, for example, "What God hath joined together..." (Matt. 19:6), was he saying that ALL couples who get married are joined by God? Even those with a strict view do not believe *all* are so joined, for they believe God only joins "first" marriages. Jesus spoke of WHAT God has joined together—by instituting marriage at the beginning—not necessarily WHOM, as though each and every couple that marries is individually joined by God.

Does God join together a couple when the marriage is based on fraud or hypocrisy? What about a woman who marries a man who did not tell her he has serious mental problems? What about a man who does not tell his wife-to-be that he has a venereal disease (which could be passed on to her or an innocent child)? What about a woman who marries a man only because he has a lot of money? Is this a basis that is honored by God when no love is present? Certainly some would have a problem believing that a black marrying a white would be joined by God. (I mention this with no prejudice against either color.) Can teen-age marriages made while in an alcoholic stupor or while drifting on a drug filled cloud of serenity measure up to the intention of God at the beginning?

According to some, God has joined together all marriages — or at least all *first* marriages — and since God has joined them, let no man put them asunder—*with no exceptions!* I don't believe this was the intent of Jesus and it baffles me that there are people who do.

WHO CAUSES ADULTERY?

Jesus taught that a man who puts away his wife *"causeth her to commit adultery"* (Matt. 5:32). This was true in many cases—enough to justify the general statement—but that ALL cases were not meant is evident, for some women who were put away remained *single.* None believe that *every* woman committed adultery simply because a man put her away. Some women in those days, in order to survive economically, were forced into prostitution — but, again, this was not true in every case. The general nature of Jesus'statement in this connection is evident.

The discussion with the Pharisees had to do with what was "lawful." Putting away for any cause and marrying "another" was termed adultery by Jesus. But, under the law, certainly not ALL men who married "another" committed adultery. In the case of polygamy, for example, a man might have several wives. Abraham, Isaac, Jacob, Gideon, David, Solomon, and, figuratively, even God himself had more than one wife (Ezekiel 23:4, 37). It is not that polygamy was ever a practical arrangement, but I point this out to show that ALL men who married "another" did not commit adultery under the law.

In the discussion, Jesus quoted from Genesis 2:24: "For this cause shall a *man* leave father and mother..." Did this mean a *man* should leave his parents, but a *woman* must not? One writer took it this way, even to stating that if a man married a woman who lived in a distant town, he must move to that town where her parents are! Of course this is not the point. We assume, and correctly so, that these words about a man leaving his parents would apply also to the woman leaving hers. Again, a basic fact of language is apparent: not ALL details are spelled out in general statements.

HARDNESS OF HEART

When the Pharisees asked about the bill of divorce, Jesus answered, "Moses because of the *hardness of your hearts* suffered you to put away your wives..." (Matt. 19:8). That many of the Jewish men had hard hearts is evident. But we must not assume that ALL men who put away their wives had hard hearts. When Joseph thought Mary had been unfaithful and

20

would have put her away, we are told he was a "just" man. He actually received revelations from God while in this frame of mind (Matt. 1:19, 20). His putting away would not have been because of hardness of heart.

An even more powerful example involves not just a man of God, but GOD HIMSELF! The language is figurative, of course, but the principle is there. "And I saw, when for all the causes whereby backsliding Israel committed adultery I had *put her away,* and given her a *bill of divorce...*" (Jer. 3:8). Would any say that the Lord had hardness of heart? Clearly the words of Jesus about hardness formed a general statement. ALL cases were not included; there were exceptions.

The passage about the "bill of divorce" — to which Jesus and the Pharisees referred — said that once a woman was given this bill, "her former husband, which sent her away, *may not take her again to be his wife,* after that she is defiled; for that is abomination before the Lord: and thou shalt not cause the land to sin" (Deut. 24:1-4). This is unmistakably stated in terms of "thou shalt not" that a former husband may not take her again. To do this would be "sin." But even this did not apply to ALL situations, as the following passage from Jeremiah 3:1 clearly shows:

"They say, If a man put away his wife, and she go from him, and become another man's, shall he return unto her again? shall not that land be greatly polluted? but thou hast played the harlot with *many* lovers; *yet return again to me,* saith the Lord."

Was there an exception here? Indeed. Love was greater than law. "And I said after she had done all these things, Turn thou unto me. But she returned not" (verse 7).

ALL CANNOT RECEIVE THIS SAYING

Finally, Matthew 19:10 ties in, for here another general statement was made and we are plainly told it did not apply to ALL men! "If the case of the man be so with his wife, it is not good to marry," the disciples said. We may not know *exactly* what the disciples had in mind, but in his reply, Jesus made it clear that *"all* men cannot receive this saying," showing that the single life was not intended for all people.

Having now carefully looked at various parts of the divorce passage (Matt. 19:3-11), it is clear that we are dealing with *general statements*. The fact that it was God who instituted marriage does not mean ALL marriages are of God. When Jesus said a man who puts away his wife causes her to commit adultery, he did not mean ALL women who are put away commit adultery. Not ALL who divorce have hard hearts, for God himself is represented as putting away his wife and giving her a bill of divorce. The same law that commanded a bill of divorce stated that a man who put away his wife was not to take her back. Yet, even this did not apply to ALL situations, for right in the very face of this law, God himself said to the wife he had put away, "Return unto me"! When the disciples spoke of the single life, Jesus clearly said this was not for "ALL men."

Now, if there were exceptions to general statements all the way through this passage, why should any insist that the statement of Jesus about divorce was not also a general statement? When Jesus said that whosoever puts away his wife and marries another commits adultery, he was speaking within the context of putting away "for every cause." For people to take this statement and attempt to apply it to ALL cases of divorce and remarriage is not very consistent. In his book *'Till Divorce Do Us Part,* Dr. R. Lofton Hudson has said that Jesus was "speaking out against a vicious custom of casual and irresponsible divorce, therefore the ideals he set forth must not be turned into universal, ironclad rules for all men and women under all circumstances."[8]

On this same point, Jay Adams has well said:

"Not everything that Jesus said about divorce applies to everyone—
or (at the very least) his words do not apply to everyone in the same
way. This is not to take anything away from Christ's words; rather,
it is to give them their true and full import. But we must not misuse
his words by applying them to that about which he never intended
to speak...Jesus was speaking within a context that must be recognized for what it was."[9]

A TEXT OUT OF CONTEXT
IS A PRETEXT

As we endeavor to apply the words of Jesus within the context that he gave them, there are those who will feel we are
trying to "explain away the Bible." They may claim that *they*
take the Bible "just as it is written!" But in taking the Bible
just as it is written, one must bear in mind that one verse can
make a general statement, another verse may clarify or explain
exceptions to that statement. A person could read Luke 1:37,
"With God nothing shall be *impossible,"* for example, and consider it an absolute. But another verse says it is *"impossible
for God to lie"* (Heb. 6:18). Each statement is true, of course,
but each must be understood *within its proper setting.*

According to Matthew 17:1, it was *"six* days" after Jesus
taught certain things that he took Peter, James, and John up
to the Mount of Transfiguration. Luke's account says it was
"about an *eight* days after these sayings" that this occurred
(Luke 9:28). Was it six days or eight days? Taking only the
one verse, a person might insist it was after SIX days. A person reading the other verse might dogmatically say it was
EIGHT days. Each would claim to be taking the Bible "just
as it is written," of course! I mention this, not because these
two verses are irreconcilable, but to show that a degree of interpretation *is* required. Conclusions should not be based on
partial evidence.

True doctrine must be based on "*every* word of God" (Matt 4:4) — not on isolated verses taken out of their proper setting Take, for example, the time the Pharisees asked Jesus for sign, tempting him. According to Mark's gospel, Jesus said "There shall NO sign be given unto this generation," and lef

"*Entering into the ship he departed to the other side*" (Mark 8:13).

in a ship (Mark 8:12). Taking this verse *alone*, it would be eas to conclude that *no sign whatsoever* was given. Period. It woul seem this was an absolute, not a general statement. But, turn ing to Matthew, who gives a more complete account, it is clea that the statement was indeed general, for there was room fc an exception: "There shall no sign be given to it [this genera tion], *but* the sign of the prophet Jonas" — the sign about thre days and three nights (Matt. 12:39, 40).

This same point may be seen concerning the statement o Jesus about divorce. According to Mark's account, Jesus sai that whosoever puts away his wife and marries another com mits adultery (Mark 10:11). This, also, would seem like a absolute. But that it was a *general* statement is clear from Mat thew's account which includes the words, "Except it be for for nication" (Matt. 19:9). Taking all that the Bible says on th subject clarifies the whole thing.

TEMPTING WITH TRICK QUESTIONS

The questions of the Pharisees about a sign from heaven, tribute to Caesar, the commandments, the woman taken in adultery, and putting away for every cause were all designed, we are told, to "tempt" Jesus. Answers given in these circumstances would not normally be considered a proper basis on which to build inflexible doctrines. In the subject before us, even if Jesus intended to totally change the Old Testament divorce law so that no remarriage under any circumstances would be allowed (as some teach), this could not be the point here. The discussion centered on what was "lawful" according to the law of Moses. And while the part about a man putting away his wife and marrying another was actually directed to the disciples later, "in the house," as Mark's account mentions, Jesus was still speaking about "the *same* matter" (Mark 10:10). The kind of divorce that was being discussed, primarily, was that sad *abuse* of the law: divorce for every cause. Those who assume that *all* kinds of divorce were condemned in this brief statement should produce evidence for this conclusion. The burden of proof rests on them.

It was not uncommon for Jesus to use strong, brief statements to drive home unfamiliar or unwelcomed truths. To take such statements in a strict, literalistic way—"just as they are written"—without the proper interpretation, could be very misleading. The following are examples:

"Take up serpents" (Mark 16:18).

"Eat the flesh of the Son of man, and drink his blood" (John 6:53).

"Be as perfect as your Father which is in heaven" (Matt. 5:48).

"Hate your father, and mother, and wife, and children" (Luke 14:26).

CONFLICTING STATEMENTS

Statements of Jesus which seemingly conflict with other

statements also require a degree of interpretation. Jesus said, "Whosoever shall say, Thou fool, shall be in danger of hell fire," yet he called people fools (Matt. 5:22, 23:17, 19). "All they that take the sword shall perish with the sword," yet in another place Jesus said, "He that hath no sword, let him buy one" (Matt. 26:52; Lk. 22:36). "When thou makest a dinner or a supper, call not thy friends," yet Jesus ate with his friends on many occasions (Lk. 14:12). "Think not that I am come to send peace on earth," yet Jesus was the "Prince of Peace," and even at his birth angels announced the idea of peace on earth (Matt. 10:34; Isaiah 9:6; Lk. 2:14).

To properly understand many of the ethical sayings of Jesus, a proper interpretation is required, as the following examples show.

"Give to him that asketh thee" (Matt. 5:42). Was this meant to apply to all situations? Would one give money to an intoxicated man so he could buy more wine? Must we give to a compulsive gambler? Must a parent give money to his children every time they ask? Should one give to high-pressure religious groups that send letters begging for money? Jesus taught that his followers should be giving and generous — *not gullible*. If we are compelled to go a mile and we go two, this does not mean we have to go twenty! (see Matt. 5:39-41). These things have their proper and scriptural limit.

"Sell all that thou hast, and distribute unto the poor" (Luke 18:22). "Take no thought for the morrow...for your life, what

"So do not worry about tomorrow" (Matt. 6:34, T.E.B.)

ye shall eat, drink nor what ye shall put on" (Matt. 6:25, 34). Suppose your daughter is married to a young man and they have two or three children. One day your son-in-law joins some extremist group that *claims* to take the teachings of Jesus literally. He sells the house he

26

and your daughter had worked to buy, gives the money away, and moves to a low rent housing area. He quits his job, taking no thought for tomorrow. No insurance is purchased, since he is not to think about the concerns of life. Things such as medical and dental care are neglected. They struggle because of a lack of food and clothing for themselves and the children. This is not victorious living! Jesus didn't tell all people to sell all they have. This challenge was directed to a man for whom possessions had become his god. When Jesus spoke of taking no thought for tomorrow, he was not advocating irresponsibility, but was saying that people should not *worry*.

"If ye ask any thing in my name, I will do it" (John 14:14). What if a Christian farmer is praying for rain for his crops on a certain day and, on that same day, another equally devout Christian is praying it will *not* rain because his family is going on a picnic? Both prayers cannot be answered. Surely "any thing" must be qualified by its compliance with the will of God (1 John 5:14).

"Make to yourselves friends of the mammon of unrighteousness; that, when ye fail, they may receive you into everlasting habitations" (Lk. 16:9). This statement must be understood as very strong *satire*. To take it at face value would be just the opposite of the over-all point of the passage: that one cannot serve God and mammon.

One final example will suffice. "If thine eye offend thee, pluck it out, and cast it from thee" (Matt. 18:9). If all church members took this saying in a literalistic way, think how many would have eyes missing! Imagine the scene at the pastor's office. Here comes Bert to talk to the pastor. He is deeply depressed. He offended with his eye and cut it out. Though he is hurting and miserable, he has obeyed the words of Jesus— literally. In a short time, Clyde rushes into the office with only one eye. He had lusted with his eyes! Would not the pastor

27

quickly explain that these words of Jesus were *not* meant to be taken in a literalistic sense?

When two harlots each claimed that a baby was hers, Solomon ordered the baby cut in two and half given to each. This was spoken, not that he intended to actually do it, but to determine which was the true mother (1 Kings 3:16-27). The point is the same in the saying of Jesus. It is not that he wants people deprived of eyes, or hands or feet—but the threat of this makes a

"Divide the living child in two"
(1 Kings 3:25).

very strong and valid point.

How does all of this tie in with our present subject — divorce and remarriage? It shows that sayings of Jesus, if not properly interpreted, can be grossly misunderstood. Those who have used the statement of Jesus about divorce to condemn *all* cases of divorce have caused much heartache and heartbreak. For some, the literalistic interpretation of these words has caused more hurt to people than if they did indeed lose an eye, foot or hand. To divorce for any cause, as some of the Jews were doing, is one thing. To say divorce is *never* permitted is the other extreme. By failing to properly interpret the words of Jesus, some have taken his words to form a new legalism.

3

"EXCEPT IT BE FOR FORNICATION"

Probably the best proof that the statement of Jesus concerning divorce and remarriage was a *general* statement — and not one meant to cover ALL cases without exception — is seen right within the text itself. Matthew's account points out a major exception — perhaps *the* major exception — to the general statement. Jesus said that a man who puts away his wife and remarries another commits adultery, *"except it be for fornication"* (Matt. 19:9). If a man puts away his wife because she has committed fornication, he is free to remarry. In this case, there is no adultery involved.

Those who insist that divorce and remarriage are *never* permitted, face a serious difficulty with this verse. Consequently, they have promoted the idea that "fornication" means sexual relations *before* marriage, *not after.* (It is claimed that a woman who is unfaithful after marriage commits *adultery,* not fornication.) As to how a man could put away his "wife" if he was not married to her, it is pointed out that Mary was called Joseph's "wife," even though they were only engaged to be married. A Jewish engagement was considered quite binding, even to the extent that when Joseph thought Mary had been untrue, he could have "put her away" (See Matthew 1:18, 19). Thus, by teaching that divorce was only permitted because of sexual sin committed *before* marriage — as during a Jewish engagement period — those who hold this view seek to rule out any and all divorce and remarriage after people are *actually* married.

It is no doubt true that the Jewish engagement was considered more binding than our custom of engagement today. It is also true that a woman engaged to a man was called his "wife"—she was his espoused wife (cf. Deut. 22:23, 24). But one should not base too much on this point. Though Matthew terms Mary as Joseph's "wife" when she was only engaged to him, he also refers to her as the "mother" of Jesus, though this was obviously before Jesus was born (Matt. 1:18). In this same sense, the writer says that Jesus begat "David the king" (verse 6), though it was many years after David was begotten that he became king. We understand, of course, that these verses were written long after these events happened. The writer simply spoke of some things from his viewpoint at the time he wrote.

NOT A JEWISH ENGAGEMENT PERIOD

But all of this talk about a Jewish engagement period is really beside the point, for what Jesus discussed with the Pharisees was *actual* marriage. When he spoke of a man putting away his wife because of fornication, there is no reason to believe he suddenly changed the subject from *actual* marriage to something different. When the Pharisees asked about the bill of divorce, the verse referred to involved *actual* marriage (Deut. 24:1-4). This bill was not merely a paper given to one who was unfaithful during a Jewish engagement period (Jer. 3:8, cf. Ezekiel 16:8, 20). And when Jesus took the discussion back further still, to the marriage of Adam and Eve, he was certainly not talking about a Jewish engagement period! The subject all the way through concerned *actual* marriage.

Those who teach that "fornication" means only sexual relations *before* marriage, may quote one definition of an English dictionary in support, but this is only in modern English, a distinction that has sometimes been used in American law. This is very unscholarly, for if we are seeking to establish what the *Bible* teaches about "fornication," we must use the word in the same sense it is used *in the Bible!*

Admittedly, when both terms — "fornication" and "adultery" — are used in the same verse (Matt. 19:9; Gal. 5:19), there must be a distinction in meaning. But this distinction is not between married and unmarried people. "Adultery" is sexual intercourse between two people — single *or* married — who are not lawfully married to each other. "Fornication" can mean adultery, but has a more *expanded* meaning, including such acts as incest, homosexuality, and prostitution. The two terms are related in meaning, yet different. In a sense, it is like the saying that all Fords are cars, but not all cars are Fords.

The Hebrew word for fornication in the Old Testament, *zanah,* is translated by such expressions as "fornication" (Isaiah 23:17), "harlot" (Josh. 6:17), "play the harlot" (Jer. 2:20), "whore" (Lev. 19:29), "whoredom" (Lev. 20:5), and "go a-whoring" (Exodus 34:15). The equivalent New Testament Greek word, *porneia,* is used of marital unfaithfulness (Matt. 19:9), incest (1 Cor. 5:1), and homosexual sins (Jude 7). *Never* is the word limited to single people!

The idea that "fornication" is committed by single people only (and "adultery" by married people) cannot be true, for *both* terms are used of the *same* person! The woman described in Ezekiel 16 who committed "adultery" also committed "fornication" [*zanah*] (verses 26, 32). The woman described in Jeremiah 3 who "played the harlot" [*zanah,* fornication], also committed "adultery" (verses 1, 8). Both terms are used in Revelation 2:21, 22: "I gave her space to repent of her *fornication;* and she repented not. Behold, I will cast her into a bed, and them that commit *adultery* with her." If fornication was an act committed by a single person and adultery an act committed by a married person, the women in all these passages would have had to be married and unmarried *at the same time!*

There is not one verse of scripture to support the idea that fornication is sexual sin committed only by *unmarried* people. On the other hand, many scriptures speak of *married* people committing fornication *(zanah)*. The prophet Ezekiel likened Jerusalem to a *married* woman with sons and daughters who "committed fornication" [*zanah*] (Ezekiel 16:26). Aholah, a *married* woman—"shall be an harlot [*zanah*] in the city" (Amos 7:17; Hosea 2:5). A *married* woman became a "harlot [*zanah*] with many lovers" and was given a bill of divorce (Jer. 3:1, 8). None of these references could possibly refer to sexual acts committed by an unmarried person. None refer to a Jewish engagement period!

During a time of extreme apostasy, "the inhabitants of Jerusalem committed fornication" [*zanah*] (2 Chron. 21:11). It would be silly to say the inhabitants of Jerusalem were all *single* people! Certainly the thousands of men who committed "whoredom" [*zanah,* fornication] with the daughters of Moab were not all single men (Numbers 25:1, 2). In referring to this event Paul said, "Neither let *us* commit fornication, as some of them committed, and fell in one day three and twenty thousand" (1 Cor. 10:8). This verse links the New Testament word translated "fornication" with the equivalent Old Testament word translated "fornication."

In the New Testament, a man who committed incest with his father's wife—a married woman—was rebuked for "fornication" (1 Cor. 5:1). Within the symbolism of Revelation, we read about "the kings of the earth who committed fornication" with the prostitute called "Mystery Babylon" (Rev. 17:2-5). Surely the kings of the earth were not all single men. Converts from among the Gentiles—thousands of them!— were told to abstain from "fornication" (Acts 15:29). We should not suppose all of these were unmarried people. These and other references show that "fornication"—whether in the Old Testament or New Testament—was never limited to single people. Those who dogmatically oppose all divorce because of their tradition, must teach an idea about the word "fornication" that is not only without scriptural support, it is contrary to the scriptures.

32

The idea that fornication meant an offense committed before marriage was not even thought of for the *first four centuries* of this era. So says the very scholarly and detailed work known as *Hasting's Encyclopedia of Religion and Ethics:* "It is a sufficient refutation of this view that such an interpretation was not thought of by the writers of the first four centuries, and that no difficulty was found in recognizing *porneia* as a general term, including in itself all sins of the flesh, and in this particular instance [Matt. 19:9] applying to adultery."[10]

"ONE FLESH"

The basic reason why fornication is just grounds for divorce is because it is a breaking apart of that which made a man and women ONE. In marriage, Jesus pointed out, two become "one flesh," quoting from Genesis 2:24. Paul, referring to this verse, said that a man who has sexual intercourse with an harlot becomes "one flesh" also. "Know ye not that he which is joined to an harlot is one body? for two, saith he, shall be one flesh" (1 Cor. 6:16). When a man becomes *one* with another woman, how can he still be *one* with his wife? By this action, an unfaithful husband severs that which made his wife and him one.

God does not require a Christian woman to forever remain with a man who is not home on Saturday nights, who is partying and carousing with prostitutes. She is not required to submit her body to his that may be infected with venereal disease that could be transmitted to her. No wonder Matthew emphasized fornication as a just cause for divorce!

Matthew includes the exception clause, not only in Matthew 19:9, but also in Matthew 5:32:

"Whosoever shall put away his wife, *saving for the cause of fornication,* causeth her to commit adultery: and whosoever shall marry her that is divorced committeth adultery."

In this verse, we are not told whether the man who puts away his wife remarries or not. Instead, the emphasis is on what he *causes*. Jesus put the blame right back where it belonged — on the man — *if* she falls into a life of adultery. I say "if," for everyone recognizes that not all women who are divorced commit adultery. A woman who never remarries and lives a chaste life could not be accused of committing adultery — not by any possible interpretation.

Some take this verse to mean that *everyone* who remarries after divorce commits adultery and *everyone* who marries a divorced person commits adultery. This cannot be true of "everyone," for it would ignore the exception clause: "saving for the cause of fornication." Suppose a marriage breaks up on the basis that one party has committed fornication and the other has not. For clarification we will call one person the "guilty" party and the other the "innocent" party. Which has the right to remarry? Certainly it is the *innocent*. If, then, an innocent woman is divorced, she does not commit adultery by getting married again nor does the man who marries her commit adultery. The exception clause allows remarriage to the innocent party.

Some get this turned around and suppose a woman guilty of fornication can be put away and remarry, but an innocent woman who is divorced cannot! This makes no sense. This would reward the guilty and punish the innocent. If this were true, a woman would only have to commit fornication, her husband would divorce her "for fornication," and she would have grounds to remarry! No, it must be understood that the exception clause provides Biblical grounds to the innocent, not the guilty. The guilty person has committed sin and must seek God's forgiveness.

The word "so" in the Weymouth translation helps express the proper sense of this verse: "But I tell you that every man who puts away his wife, except on the ground of unchastity, causes her to commit adultery, and whoever marries her when *so* divorced commits adultery."[11] A man who marries a woman "so divorced"—because of fornication—commits adultery. If the woman was innocent, there could be no adultery involved. As John Calvin, the noted theologian and reformer, wrote: "Though Christ condemns as an adulterer the man who shall marry a wife that has been divorced, this is undoubtedly restricted to *unlawful and frivolous divorces.*"[12] Even the highly regarded *Pulpit Commentary* agrees with this conclusion: "Our Lord does not say that the remarriage of divorced persons is in ALL cases adulterous."[13]

FOOD FOR THOUGHT

Though it is not an essential point, it may be of interest to Bible students to include the following details about Matthew 5:32. The word translated "divorced" in the phrase "whosoever shall marry her that is *divorced* committeth adultery," is nowhere else so translated in the Bible. The Greek word used here is *apoluo,* the correct translation being "put away" as it is translated in the parallel places. (The Greek word for divorce is a different word.) The word *apoluo* appears 69 times and is translated as follows: "depart" (three times), "loose" (two times), "dismiss" (two times), "set at liberty" (two times), "forgive" (two times), "send away" (thirteen times), "let go" (thirteen times), "release" (seventeen times), "put away" (fourteen times), and "divorced" only this one time! "Divorced" is obviously not the best translation here.

Though a man who divorces his wife also puts her away, as it were, the expression "put away" does not mean the same as divorce. This can be seen in the following verses in which I have substituted "divorce" where *apoluo* is used: "And when he had *divorced* the multitudes, he went up into a mountain to pray" (Matt. 14:23). "Woman thou art *divorced* from thine infirmity" (Luke 13:12). "Pilate said unto them, whom will ye that I *divorce* unto you?" (Matt. 27:17). "Will ye therefore that

35

I *divorce* unto you the King of the Jews?" (John 18:39), etc.

The fact that Moses required a bill of *divorce* to be given to a woman who was *put away,* shows that the two are not one and the same. Sometimes women were merely put away — kicked out, driven from the house, or deserted — without being given a legal bill of divorce. Some of the hardhearted men of Jesus' day may have been doing this. In these circumstances, a woman who married again committed adultery (at least in a *legal* sense), as did the man who married her, because she was only "put away," not divorced. So it is understood in the Lamsa version, a translation from the Aramaic which many believe was the language that Jesus spoke: "...and whoever marries a woman who is *separated but not divorced,* commits adultery" (Matt. 5:32). This explanation is not without some merit and possibility, but it is not essential to our over-all theme.

EXCEPTIONS EVEN TO COMMANDMENTS

Since "fornication" is mentioned as an exception to the statement of Jesus about divorce and remarriage, we know the statement was general in nature. What many have not understood is that statements in the Bible, even "commandments," can have *exceptions.* Take, for example, the commandment "Thou shalt not steal" (Exodus 20:15). This seems conclusive enough, yet *all* details are not explained in these four words. What if a man did steal, then what? Two chapters later this is explained: "If a man shall steal an ox...and kill it, or sell it; he shall restore five oxen for an ox" (Exodus 22:1).

Before leaving Egypt, the Israelites "borrowed" jewels, silver, gold, and clothing from the Egyptians, *knowing* they were not going to return the merchandise (Exodus 3:22)! Was it stealing? Technically, as slaves they had earned more than they were paid. But in the eyes of the Egyptians, at least, this "borrowing" was certainly stealing!

An Israelite was allowed to eat grapes from his neighbor's vineyard as he passed by, but he was not to put any in a con-

tainer (Deut. 23:24). Even though he took something that was not his, this was not considered stealing. A man today who grows grapes, however, might not see it that way!

Stealing done by a man who does so to preserve his life or that of his family in adverse circumstances is not looked on as severly as someone who steals only for material gain. Even Proverbs 6:30 says, "Men do not despise a thief, if he steal to satisfy his soul when he is hungry." The point is, all

"Thou mayest eat grapes...but thou shalt not put any in thy vessel" (Deut. 23:24).

details are not totally explained in the four words, "Thou shalt not steal."

ALL IMAGES FORBIDDEN?

Then there is the commandment, "Thou shalt not make unto thee *any* graven image, or any likeness of *anything"* (Exodus 20:4). This commandment was a strong warning against idolatry. But for any to believe God *never* permitted "images" or "likenesses" to be made, reveals a degree of Biblical ignorance. Even Moses himself, through whom this commandment was given, made an image of a snake out of brass which he lifted up in the sight of the people. When they looked to this image in faith, they were healed (Numbers 21:9).

Moses committed no sin when he set up twelve pillars and offered sacrifices (Exodus 24:2); though pillars dedicated to heathen gods were strongly condemned (Deut. 12:3). When the Israelites made a golden *calf*, a great sin was committed (Exodus 32:8); yet, within the very temple of God, a huge basin rested upon statues of twelve *oxen* (1 Kings 7:24-26). Two different sets of circumstances were involved, obviously, even though each involved making an image.

"Neither be ye idolaters, as were of them" (1 Cor. 10:7).

Also within the temple were likenesses of hundreds of pomegranates on pillars with lily work (1 Kings 7:18, 19, 42). The cherubim, apparently similar in some ways to the winged bulls with human heads of Assyrian mythology, were images that stood over the holy ark of the convenant (Exodus 25:18-22). Images of fruit, flowers, and trees were also used (Numbers 8:4; 1 Kings 6:18; 7:36). The king's throne rested on fourteen carved lions (1 Kings 10:19, 20). Thus, the command which would seem to absolutely forbid the making of any likeness of men, animals, or plants, is seen to be a general statement to which there were scriptural exceptions. It was not an absolute and universal prohibition.

THE SABBATH

The sabbath commandment required that no work be done on this day (Exodus 20:10). Were there exceptions to this? Yes; and we have this on the very authority of Jesus himself. When some of the strict people criticized the disciples for picking corn on the sabbath, Jesus replied:

> "Have ye not read what David did when he was an hungred... how he entered into the house of God, and did eat the shewbread, which was *not lawful* for him to eat... but only for the priests?" (Matt. 12:4).

All of this ties in, for it was on the sabbath that David had done this! The sacred bread was kept continually on a table in the Lord's presence, fresh bread being prepared by the priests every sabbath to replace the bread which had been there through the previous week (Num. 4:7; 1 Chron. 9:32; Lev. 24:8). It was when this sacred bread "was taken from before the Lord, to put hot bread *in the day when it was taken"* — on the sabbath — that David ate this bread that was lawful only for priests (1 Sam. 21:6). By pointing this out, if Jesus was not teaching that in certain circumstances there are *exceptions* to laws, what was he saying?

Was it possible for some to do work on the sabbath — to actually profane the sabbath — and yet be blameless? Absolutely. Notice what Jesus went on to say:

> "Or have ye not read in the law, how that on the sabbath days the priests in the temple *profane* the sabbath [by doing the labor of killing sacrifices, baking shewbread, etc. — Numbers 28:9, 10; 1 Chron. 9:32], and are *blameless?"* (Matt. 12:5).

It was necessary for these priests to break one commandment, *as it were*, in order to keep another. This is a problem area for the legalists who fail to recognize that one rule does not necessarily apply to all people in all situations. The speed limit may be 55 miles an hour, yet in order to enforce this law, a police officer may have to go 90 miles an hour to catch the offender. It is not that the officer is above the law, it is not that the law is wrong, it is simply that general rules or laws can have exceptions.

The Israelites were commanded to march around the city of Jericho — a march much longer than the lawful sabbath day's journey—and this was to be carried out for *seven* days. One of these days *had* to fall on the sabbath! (Joshua 6:1-16). Even the Jews recognized that sometimes one law superseded another, as when a male child was circumcised on the eighth day of his life. If this happened to fall on the sabbath, the law of circumcision was considered superior to the sabbath (John 7:22).

"I have given into thine hand Jericho" (Joshua 6:2).

WAS ALL KILLING UNLAWFUL?

There were even exceptions to the law "Thou shalt not kill" (Exodus 20:13). The Hebrews killed their enemies during wars. They killed their own people—3,000 of them in one day who worshipped the golden calf (Exodus 32:27, 28). They killed blasphemers, disobedient sons, criminals, heretics, and sex perverts. As they conquered new land, they killed people—old and young, male and female. They killed animals for sacrifices. All of this killing was done in obedience to Moses, the very one to whom the commandment "thou shalt not kill" is attributed! Not to kill was a general statement; there were exceptions.

We believe this was also the case with the saying of Jesus against divorce and remarriage. As a *general* statement there was room for an exception. Matthew expressly mentioned "fornication" as an exception. But just because only one exception is mentioned in this text, there is no reason to conclude this is the *only* exception. Other verses, as we shall notice in more detail later, mention other exceptions.

40

ONE EXCEPTION ONLY?

The Biblical account of the Pharisees asking for a sign provides an example of a statement being made, one exception being mentioned, and yet the meaning is definitely not limited to only one exception. Mark's account says, "There shall no sign be given" (Mark 8:12). Matthew records an exception to this: "There shall no sign be given, but the sign of the prophet Jonah"—about him being three days and three nights in the belly of the whale (Matt. 12:39, 40). But this was not the *only* exception, for Luke (11:29, 30) records yet another sign—about Jonah himself being a sign to the Ninevites (this was *after* the whale episode). Actually, there were *many* signs that Jesus gave to that generation—*not just one* (Acts 2:22; Heb. 2:3, 4; John 4:48-50; 20:30; Luke 2:12, etc.). The mention of an exception following words like "except" or "but" does not necessarily mean that such is the *only* exception.

As an example of this point, I have purposely included the following text, for it appears—at first glance—to allow only one exception. It uses the expression *"all*...but," yet even with this strong wording there may be room for more than one exception. *"All* manner of sin and blasphemy shall be forgiven unto men; but the blasphemy against the Holy Ghost shall not be forgiven unto men" (Matt. 12:31). We commonly use the expression *"the* unpardonable sin"—as though there is only one. But is this really what Jesus said?

What about a man who does not blaspheme the Holy Ghost—does not attribute the works of Christ to Satan (verses 24-31)—but who fails to receive Christ as savior and dies in his sin? Is failure to receive Christ—the sin of unbelief—a sin that will not be forgiven? What if a man commits murder and does not repent? The Bible says no murderer shall enter the kingdom of heaven. Imagine a man who for an excuse might say, "The only sin God won't forgive is blasphemy against the Holy Ghost. So I can commit murder, idolatry, fornication,

41

adultery, perversion, and finally commit suicide and still be forgiven—in this world or the next—just as long as I don't blaspheme the Holy Ghost!" This is unthinkable. Jesus mentioned an exception, but this does not rule out the possibility of other exceptions—not in this passage or the one about divorce and remarriage! We should not read the word "only" into verses that were not intended to have that meaning.

The idea that fornication is the only basis for divorce actually *caused* fornication in the following true incident!

> For years Don and Edna had faced serious difficulties in their marriage. Edna was a Christian; Don was not. They talked about divorce at different times, but being a Christian, Edna explained why she felt she could not divorce. "Don, according to the Bible, I cannot divorce and remarry 'except it be for fornication,' and since you have not done this, I have no grounds!" Don's answer was quite simple: "If that is all that is standing in the way, I can oblige you; I will commit fornication." The following Saturday night he made arrangements with a local prostitute, giving his wife "grounds"!

If fornication is the *only* exception to the statement of Jesus about divorce and remarriage, many questions would remain unanswered. It would not settle the problem for multitudes of devout people who have agonized about their standing with God because of a previous marriage. Is a husband unfaithful to his wife only if he has sexual intercourse with another woman? Is he not unfaithful if he lies and deceives her? Or what if he does things *worse* than fornication?

A man who committed fornication in a weak moment, might repent of it and never repeat it. There would be hurts, but a wife could forgive him and happiness be restored. That situation could not possibly be as bad as that of a woman who lives in misery day after day, year after year, being mistreated, belittled, and abused by her husband—*even though no fornication is committed.*

42

CRIMES WORTHY OF DEATH

Within the Old Testament law, an unfaithful wife was to be stoned to death, or she could be *divorced*. We have the example of God himself who divorced his unfaithful wife Israel rather than having her killed (Jer. 3:8) and of Joseph who, when he thought Mary had been untrue, would have taken this same option—divorce (Matt. 1:19). When a wife was stoned to death, the husband was automatically free to marry again. When divorce was substituted for death, *this same right to remarry remained*. It follows, then, that crimes worthy of death—bestiality (Exodus 22:19), rape (Deut. 22:25, 26), murder (Exodus 21:12, 14), idolatry (Lev. 18:23), etc.—could also provide sufficient grounds for divorce and remarriage. Whether the death penalty was actually carried out is beside the point. Many of these crimes were *worse* than fornication!

Suppose a man in our day committed a horrible crime and was executed for it. His wife would be free to remarry—of course. But what if this *same* man, married to the *same* woman, commits the *same* crime in a state that does not have the death penalty? In a state like Michigan (which abolished the death penalty in 1847), for example, he might spend the rest of his life in prison. Missouri, on the other hand, still retains the death penalty. If the man committed the crime in Michigan, he would not be executed, but could be in Missouri! Are we to conclude, then, that his wife (if she remarried) would be committing adultery just because *he* committed a crime in *Michigan* instead of *Missouri?* The legalist might insist on this. But whether one state carries out the death penalty and another does not, the crime is still the same in the sight of God. Remarriage would be the women's right regardless; God's justice is not short circuited by state lines!

It might be impossible for a man locked up in prison for life to commit adultery. But this would not mean his *heart* would not be filled with all sorts of lust. Since God looks on the heart, he could be an adulterer in the sight of God. Those who believe in one exception *only* might fail to see any grounds here, since no act is *literally* committed. They seem to ignore the fact that adultery can be committed in one's heart (Matt. 5:28). They fail to recognize that one thing can be the *equivalent* of another. I am reminded of the words of a pastor: "Only *adultery,* not *absence,* is grounds for divorce!" He was talking to a woman whose husband had deserted her. Even though it had been five years since she knew where he was, this made no difference the way this pastor had it figured!

Surely if fornication is sufficient grounds for divorce and remarriage, we should not rule out the possibility of things that are worse than fornication being counted as the same — things such as attempted murder — as in the following true story:

> While on a visit to some relatives, a fine Christian girl met a young man who courted her and won her heart and hand. They married and moved to a little farm. When she became pregnant a few months later, the husband worked out a scheme to kill her. After hitting her in the head with a heavy object, he threw her down into the cellar, breaking a jar of cream in front of her to make it appear she fell accidently. The circumstantial evidence seemed perfect. He quickly rushed from the scene, planning to return later and report the death. After he left, however, she regained consciousness. Smeared with blood, she managed to crawl back up the stairs and over to a neighbor's home for help. The husband was arrested and sent to prison for a period of time. The woman obtained a divorce, later remarried, and established a happy home.

Since this man had not committed "fornication," those who suppose this is the *only* exception might tell this woman she was "living in adultery" (an expression the Bible never uses!) or they might even say she should divorce her second husband and remain single — just in case her first husband should repent and want to come back to her!

4

"FORBIDDING TO MARRY"

The marriage has ended in divorce. A return to the former marriage is out of the question. A person finds himself single, alone. Where does he go from here? Does the Bible "forbid to marry" in these circumstances? Does it require celibacy for divorced people?

In his discussion with the Pharisees, Jesus pointed out that it was God who instituted marriage in the beginning. At that time, we recall, God had said: "It is not good that the man should be *alone*" (Gen. 2:18). So he made Eve and she and Adam became husband and wife. Now suppose there had been another man in the world and, in the course of time, Eve went off to live with him, leaving Adam again "alone." Would these circumstances then make it "good" for Adam to be alone? Could some evil that Eve did change that which was "good" for Adam?

Without thinking this through, some assume that it is not "good" for a man to be "alone" — *if he has never been married.* But if he was formerly married, then God requires him to be alone the rest of his life — that it is "good" for a divorced man to be "alone"! But why? What purpose is served by requiring anyone to live in celibacy? Is it some form of *penance* for past mistakes? Must one stay single to make *his own atonement,* as it were, for wrongs committed? Have people who teach such things forgotten that, even if sin was involved, God *forgives* sin? *Why* should a person who has suffered failure in marriage be forbidden to pick up the pieces and, with God's help, make a new start in life?

Some years ago I knew a young man who had an outstanding conversion. Old things passed away and all things became new. His wife, however, did not go along with this change in his life—not at all. She soon left him, caring nothing at all about trying to live "right." Adding to his feeling of loss was the fact that a child had already been born into the marriage. The young man was only 19! The church in which he was converted was one that teaches celibacy—*for divorced people*. They told him he could never marry again, that he must remain single the rest of his life. He had a deep desire to go on with the Lord and assumed that this unnatural celibacy was God's requirement. I don't know what ever happened to him, but we can only ask why God would want to punish *him* for what *someone else did*. This is not the way God works.

Jesus taught that marriage—not divorce—was the original ideal. But if divorce does occur, why should we assume the teaching of Jesus requires all divorced persons to remain forever single? This can hardly be the case. In the very *same* passage in which he spoke out against that type of divorce and remarriage that had become so abusive in his day, he added these words about the single life: *"All* men cannot receive this saying, save they to whom it is given" (Matt. 19:11). Clearly, he did not expect "all men" to live in celibacy—whether single or divorced. As Dr. Hudson has written:

> "If 'all men cannot receive this saying' applies to the never married, *how much more* would it apply to the formerly married! After a person has been accustomed to the warmth, closeness, sexual intercourse, and even companionship of marriage, it is unlikely that the savior would have condemned him to a life of aloneness and sexual abstinence."[15]

ROMISH CELIBACY

"Forbidding to marry" was called a "doctrine of devils" by Paul (1 Tim. 4:1-3). History records many cases of priests and even popes of the Roman Catholic church who fell into immorality because this doctrine was forced on them. I have given a detailed account of this immorality with references to recognized historical sources in my book *Babylon Mystery Religion*.[16] Protestants (and many Catholics) recognize the error of priestly celibacy. They know its awful history. Yet, those who hold the no-remarriage concept teach this same error — not just for priests — but for *large segments of the population!* According to their view, all of the thousands of people who have had a previous marriage should never be allowed to marry again!

This doctrine places a man in the same religious strait jacket as a Roman Catholic priest, but with one major difference: the priest *chose* to be a priest. A man with a previous marriage may not have chosen to be single. His wife may have left him. It is not very consistent for some to criticize Romanism with its doctrine of "forbidding to marry" and turn right around in the guise of an artificial holiness and teach what amounts to the same thing. Trying to force all people with a previous marriage to live in an unnatural celibacy is contrary to the statement of Jesus that the single life was not for "all men." It is contrary to the scripture that says, "It is not good that the man should be alone."

ATTEMPTED SUICIDE

Let me tell you the experience of a pastor I know. Years ago his wife left him for another man and moved to a different state. He was left with the responsibility of their two teen-age children. Belonging to an organization which did not allow remarriage, he believed that God required him to live in celibacy. He did this for a number of years, but when the children were grown and gone, he became especially lonely and fought times of deep depression. "Very late one rainy night," he told me, "I prepared weights to tie to my body and drove to a bridge which crosses the Columbia River, planning to take my life. I had every intention of doing this, but then at the last moment, as it were, I returned back to the house." The story has a happy ending, however, for a short time later he met and married a fine Christian woman who filled the void in his life. This was over twenty years ago now. He came to understand that God does not require celibacy. It was definitely *not* "good" for this man to be alone!

Martin Luther pointed out that it was *unscriptural* to require a minister or priest to be unmarried. He also opposed the idea that divorced people must remain single. "Christ permitted divorce in case of fornication and *compelled no one to remain single;* and Paul preferred us to marry rather than to burn, and seemed quite prepared to grant that a man may marry another woman in place of the one he has repudiated."[17]

In his book *Getting Married Again,* Pastor Bob W. Brown has said:

> "Candidly, I am confident that I would remarry if I were to become single. My personal life has been so involved and influenced by my marriage that I cannot easily imagine being unmarried. There is nothing about being single that appeals to me. I am not good alone. I want to share, talk, and laugh with someone. I do not want to eat alone, or weep alone, or dream alone. I am conditioned to the marriage experience. I am sure that if I were widowed or divorced I would want to marry again. Because of this, I cannot tell someone who is single, whether divorced or not, that they should not marry. They certainly have the same privileges under God that I would take for myself."[18]

Requiring a person to remain forever single following the breakup of marriage does not glorify God. A man who is taught the celibacy idea may determine to stay single. Because of loneliness or for economic reasons he may move into an apartment with another single man. There will be those who are sure he is a homosexual! They may take part in a whisper campaign, even suggesting that this must be why his wife left him! If he establishes any friendships with women, the modern Pharisees will figure he is a woman chaser. The doctrine of forced celibacy has pushed people into a corner in which they are condemned if they do, they are condemned if they don't. It is a perplexing situation — as though a man fled from a lion and a bear met him — or possibly escaping from these, leans against a wall and a snake bites him! (cf. Amos 5:19).

"As if a man did flee from a lion ...a bear...a serpent" (Amos 5:19).

When Jesus offered the water of life to the Samaritan woman who had been married and divorced five times, it was not offered on the basis that she would be required to live in celibacy! Even to the woman "taken in adultery" that the strict people would have stoned to death, Jesus said, "neither do I condemn thee: go, and sin no more." Had his teaching required celibacy, at this point he should have explained that to "sin no more" meant she must live single the rest of her life. No, this was not the teaching of Jesus.

A TEEN-AGE MARRIAGE

Let me tell you the case of Fay, a seventeen year old girl whose life at home was very difficult. Her father had a serious drinking problem and never stayed with a job very long. There were eight children and often not enough food to go around. The house they rented was in a bad part of town, was always cluttered, and life was a constant turmoil. In these circumstances, feeling unloved and unwanted, Fay met a man who was at least ten years older than her. Hoping to escape from a miserable environment, she drove with this man to Las Vegas and they were married.

She knew almost nothing of what was involved in marriage — not even cooking and basic responsibilities. Her ideas about sex were vague. Six months later the man left her —

never to return. With no money, and pregnant, which way could she turn? She considered suicide. She considered returning to the home she had left. It occured to her that she could seek out a minister for advice. The first one she contacted was a legalist who taught the doctrine of "forbidding to marry." She was told she would have to remain single — that any hope for a husband and home was evil. Fortunately, in a second attempt, she contacted a church that was progressive enough to face the reality of divorce and deal with it objectively.

I know a man — he even did some preaching at one time — whose first marriage broke up with some fault, apparently, on both sides. He was left with several children to raise. In the discouragement of it all, he drifted away from his church association and eventually remarried. The woman he married raised his children and they had a child of their own. A number of years later, with most of the children now grown and gone, they both got back into church. Regretfully, a lot of guilt and condemnation was heaped on them. The woman's former husband was dead, but the man's former wife was still living — *somewhere!* Because of the taboo some associate with such situations, they were accused of "living in adultery." They decided to remain together in a "brother-sister" relationship — he had his bedroom, she had hers. Sometimes they would go for weeks or months in this manner, only to "backslide" for a night! All of this guilt, this self-defeating concept, was unnecessary, for God forces celibacy on no one.

CORINTHIAN CELIBACY?

Some feel that Paul discouraged marriage when writing to the Christians at Corinth (1 Cor. 7). However, to what extent this may be true, such was not on moral grounds, but eschatological and practical. That is, he believed persecutions and tribulations were on the horizon for the church there. Since Christianity was not a government-recognized religion, there was no state protection as we know it today. Those who married and started families at that time might face special problems because of the circumstances. It is generally recognized that certain things Paul wrote to the Christians at Corinth must be understood in view of that "present distress" (1 Cor. 7:26).

Paul did recognize that within the human family there are some who may not be Christians and yet find the single life totally acceptable. And, on the other hand, there are Christians, *dedicated* Christians, who simply would not function at their best level in the single state. "Every man hath his proper gift of God," he wrote, "one after this manner, and another after that" (1 Cor. 7:7). *Only* those who had the gift of living the single life were told to do so. No one was *forbidden* to marry.

Though Paul favored the single life for himself (1 Cor. 7:7), apparently all the other apostles married (1 Cor. 9:5). Peter was most definitely a married man, for he had a mother-in-law! (Matt. 8:14). Instead of Paul considering marriage as an inferior state, he even used it as a type of the union between Christ and the church (Eph. 5:25-32). This would have been a poor comparison if marriage was not God-ordained. Marriage was considered honorable: "Marriage is honorable in all, and the bed undefiled" (Heb. 13:4).

Instead of forbidding marriage, notice what Paul said about marriage—including the sexual part of marriage—when writing to the Corinthians:

"To avoid fornication, let *every man* have his own wife, and let *every woman* have her own husband. Let the husband render unto the wife due benevolence: and likewise also the wife unto the husband. The wife hath not power of her own body, but the husband: and likewise also the husband hath not power of his own body, but the wife. Defraud ye not one the other, except it be with consent for a time, that ye may give yourselves to fasting and prayer; and come together again, that Satan tempt you not for your incontinency" (1 Cor. 7:2-5).

Being a very immoral city, to commit fornication at Cor-

51

inth would have been easy to do. A pagan temple dedicated to worship of the most shameful character had a thousand female slaves who were maintained for ritual prostitution. The general population did not frown on prostitution—it was even a part of their religion! Night and day there was a temptation present for temporary sexual experiences. A word the Greeks used in referring to a life of sexual depravity was *korinthiazesthai*, meaning "to carry on like a Corinthian." Considering this background, Paul's words to the Corinthians about avoiding fornication are especially weighty.

In order to avoid fornication, Paul said to let *"every* man" and *"every* woman" be married. Did these instructions about "every man" include a man who had been previously married and now was single? Certainly. Fornication would be just as much a temptation to a man who had been married before—*if not more so*—than a man who had never been married. In either case, the married state was recommended by Paul. When he said, "But I speak this by permission, and not of commandment" (verse 6), he simply meant (as *The Living Bible* phrases it), "I'm not saying you *must* marry; but you certainly *may* if you wish." Marriage was not contrary to Christian principles.

Years ago I knew a young woman with two children who was deserted by her husband and left with no support. She had a chance to marry a fine young man who had a genuine concern and love for her, but her church (in which I was holding evangelistic meetings at the time!) did not allow "second marriage." Her pastor said she must remain single—that she could never remarry. As ridiculous as this is, neither she nor her pastor knew any better. They supposed the Bible was against divorce "from Genesis to Revelation." She tried to live the single life, but instead of any positive good being accomplished by this forced celibacy, in time she actually fell into *prostitution* in order to survive and feed her children!

Paul was more sensible by far. He clearly said, "To avoid

fornication…let *every* woman have her own husband." This would include a woman whose marriage ended in divorce. Requiring her to stay single would have no purpose.

WHAT DID PAUL MEAN?

Realizing that the Bible never requires celibacy, some have wondered what Paul meant in 1 Corinthains 7:10, 11 — the part about a woman remaining unmarried.

> "And unto the married I command, yet not I, but the *Lord,* Let not the wife depart from her husband: but and if she depart, *let her remain unmarried,* or be reconciled to her husband: and let not the husband put away his wife."

Paul was here referring back to the general teaching of the Lord Jesus — a wife is not to depart from her husband and a husband is not to put away his wife. But as he wrote, possibly thinking of some unbearable situations, he added these words (which some translations put in parentheses): "…but and if she depart, let her remain unmarried, or be reconciled to her husband." From these few words, some have concluded that *all* women who go through a divorce, if they cannot be reconciled to their husbands, must forever remain single. They assume it is a closed case. I don't think we should be too quick to draw this conclusion. This is reading more into the text than was intended.

First of all, there is no reason to assume this woman who departed had *divorced.* It is true that people who divorce do indeed depart, but the word translated "depart," *chorizo,* does not necessarily mean divorce. It is a *common* word used of Paul *departing* from Athens (Acts 18:1), Jews *departing* from Rome (Acts 18:2), disciples *departing* from Jerusalem (Acts 1:4), etc. It is translated "separate" in Romans 8:35: "Who shall *separate* us from the love of Christ?" Apparently what Paul had in mind was a case in which a woman was separated, but not divorced, from her husband. Being separated, she was living in an "unmarried" state, but the man she had departed from was still called "her husband" (1 Cor. 7:11). Had she been actually divorced from him, he would have been more correctly termed her "former husband" (cf. Deut. 24:4). The fact that Paul spoke of the possibility of "reconciliation" implies that neither party had remarried. At this point it was *separation only*.

It was in *this* situation that Paul spoke of her remaining "unmarried"—not that she must remain single *forever!* Paul had just said, "I say therefore to the unmarried...if they cannot contain, let them marry" and that "every" woman had the right to be married (verses 2, 8, 9). The single life was recommended only for those who had a gift to be their best in this state. If a woman did not have this gift *before* she married, if she did not have this gift *during* marriage, why should we suppose after leaving her husband she would suddenly lose her desire for physical affection? Would Paul say that women who had physical desires for marriage *should* marry in one breath, and then turn right around and require all women who were separated from their husbands to remain unmarried *forever?*

Paul's recommendation that a woman in this situation remain unmarried was no doubt intended on a *temporary* basis—with the possibility of reconciliation to her husband being in view. To read the idea of "forever" into this verse is unwarranted. If the woman had gotten out of an unbearable situation, her remaining unmarried for a period of time would allow the husband "space to repent" (cf. Rev. 2:21). This time could allow for healing, for both parties concerned to weigh things, to try to patch things up so that reconciliation might follow. But if it became evident that reconciliation was impossible, there would be no purpose for her to stay single.

If the separation led to divorce and the husband married someone else, for example, reconciliation would be out of the question. Paul would not tell her to be reconciled to him then, for such would either constitute *bigamy* or require *another divorce* for him to take her back! Or, if the woman remarried, once it had gone this far, Paul would not suggest reconciliation, for this too would require another divorce. Besides, Deuteronomy 24:4 points out that once a woman had actually remarried, she was not to return to her former husband.

Some radicals, who apparently know little about sound rules of Biblical interpretation, take Paul's words about a woman who separated from her husband to mean she had actually *divorced,* then conclude that each woman who is divorced — even if her former husband has *remarried* — must remain *forever single!* This is unfortunate. They are reading things into this verse that are contrary to other statements in this very *same* chapter. "Forbidding to marry" was *not* the doctrine of Paul (1 Tim. 4:1-3).

5

QUESTIONS FROM CORINTHIAN CONVERTS

When Paul answered questions from the Corinthians about marriage (1 Cor. 7), he assured them that being a Christian did not require them to break up their marriages. Even though many of them no doubt had previous marriages, none were told to break up in order to return to a former marriage or to live in celibacy. The present state of marriage at the time of conversion was accepted. "Let not the wife depart from her husband...and let not the husband put away his wife," Paul said, pointing out that these words were based on a command of "the Lord" (1 Cor. 7:10, 11). When he went on to say, "But to the rest speak I, not the Lord," he meant that what he was about to say—though this too was inspired—was not based on an actual quotation from Jesus.

It is evident that Paul considered the statement of Jesus as *general* in nature (the point we made earlier, pp. 8-23), for in speaking of the "rest" of the matter, he continued by dealing with *exceptions* and *specifics*! Had he considered the statement of Jesus as an *absolute*—as though it condemned *all* cases of divorce and remarriage—he could have simply quoted the statement and been done with it. No divorce *ever*. Period. But there were exceptions. Charles B. Williams, noted Bible translator, says that the statement was "a *general* law of Christian teaching, to emphasize the sanctity of marriage; but see *exceptions* in Mt. 5:32; 19:9; also *next verses*."[19]

As we look at these "next verses," these "exceptions" to the *general* statement, Paul deals with the situation in which a believer is married to an unbeliever. The Corinthian converts had apparently asked something like this: "What about some of us, Paul, who are married to unbelievers? Is a Christian sinning by having sexual relations with an unbeliever? Must a Christian put away an unbelieving mate?" To this type of questioning, Paul replied:

> "*If* any brother hath a wife that believeth not, and she be *pleased* to dwell with him, let him not put her away. And the woman which hath an husband that believeth not, and *if* he be *pleased* to dwell with her, let her not leave him" (1 Cor. 7:12, 13).

If the Christian position was that *no* putting away was *ever* allowed, these would be strange words indeed! Why would Paul say not to put away an unbelieving wife *"if* she be pleased to dwell with him," if no divorce was *ever* permitted? If putting away was out of the question, whether she was "pleased" or "not pleased" would be beside the point! The fact that Paul used the word "if" shows there was an option. If the unbeliever was not pleased to dwell with the believer — if there was constant strife, turmoil, unhappiness, resentment, and confusion — Paul certainly did not require them to stay together in misery. We know this, for he goes right on to say that if the unbeliever departs, the believer is *no longer bound!*

> "But if the unbelieving depart, *let him depart.* A brother or a sister is *not under bondage* in such cases: but God hath called us to peace" (1 Cor. 7:15).

"*...not under bondage*"
(1 Cor. 7:15).

The word "bondage" here is translated from a Greek word that was used to describe one who was bound as a slave — the terms "under bondage" and "not under bondage" being established legal terms that were used in slave trade. If a slave was no longer under

ondage, he had been set free. The slave owner had no fur-
her claim to him. So here, applied to marriage, a person who
vas no longer "under bondage" was free from that marriage.
n his scholarly *Word Studies in the New Testament*, M.R.
Vincent has said this is "a strong word, indicating that Christianity has not made marriage a state of slavery to be-
ievers...the meaning clearly is that wilful desertion on the
part of the unbelieving husband or wife sets the other party
free."[20]

Using a general point of the law as an illustration, Paul said
a woman "was *bound* by the law to her husband so long as
he liveth" (Rom. 7:2). But here the same apostle, in different
circumstances, says that a wife is *not bound* to an unbelieving
husband who leaves her. If being "bound" in the one case meant
she was *not free* from the marriage, it is certain that her being
"*not* bound" in the second case, means she was *free* from the
marriage. If this does not mean she is free to remarry, words
have lost all meaning.

After quoting from or referring to a host of standard sources
such as Vine's *Expository Dictionary of New Testament Words,*
*The Vocabulary of the Greek New Testament, A Patristic
Greek Lexicon, Thayer's Greek English Lexicon, The New
Testament in Greek* by Westcott and Hort, and others, Guy
Duty says:

"We conclude from this evidence that 'not under bondage' expressed
the *total release* from the marital bond, and that the Greek divorce
bill *biblion apostasion* contained the same legal meaning of absolute
dissolution as did the Jewish bill...If this evidence is not sufficient
to convince a reasonable mind, then there is an end to all meaning
in language and we must despair of ever proving anything."[21]

The translator of the *Concordant Bible,* A. E. Knoch, says
in his note on this verse (1 Cor. 7:15), "The believer is to make
no move toward separation, but if the unbeliever obtains a
divorce the believer is *entirely free.*" Moffatt has translated

it: "...in such cases the Christian brother or sister is not *tied to marriage*." In his *Annotated Reference Bible*, Finis Dake has given this comment on this verse:

> "Here we have another legal and scriptural reason for divorce *and remarriage*. If the unbeliever refuses to live with a wife or husband because of Christianity and if he or she is determined to leave on this account, the Christian is not held responsible or punished by requirements to remain single the rest of his or her life because of the rebellion of another."[22]

Adam Clarke says that when an unbeliever departs, "a Christian man or woman is not under bondage to any particular laws, so as to be prevented from *remarrying*,"[23] and Martin Luther says, "Here the apostle rules that the unbeliever who deserts his wife should be divorced, and he pronounces the believer *free to marry another*."[24] Numerous reformers preachers, scholars, and Bible reference works could be quoted that make this same point. It is not a private interpretation

MARITAL MISSIONARIES?

Some Christians suppose they are required to remain in bad marriages because they may be able to save their unbelieving husband or wife. They think this is based on the following verse: "For what knowest thou, O wife, whether thou shalt save thy husband? or how knowest thou, O man, whether thou shalt save thy wife?" (1 Cor. 7:16). Notice the question marks

While it is true that a believing wife can have a positive and godly influence on an unbelieving husband (1 Peter 3:1, 2) simply staying with him does not guarantee that he will be saved. Paul was *not* saying one should stay with an unbelieving mate simply because the possibility exists of his conversion After just saying *in the verse before* that if the unbeliever departs, "let him depart," he was not turning around in this verse and saying "don't let him depart"! Notice also that the

60

word "for" introduces this verse, definitely linking it with the previous verse. Paul was saying, in effect, that the Christian is no longer bound if the unbeliever wants to depart; she should not feel she must try to remain with him; she has no way to know she could save him.

The Living Bible, though a paraphrase, gives the intended sense: "For, after all, there is no assurance to you wives that your husbands will be converted if they stay; and the same may be said to you husbands concerning your wives." This is the meaning given also in the Revised Standard, Concordant, Douay, Modern Language, Panin, Lamsa, Rotherham, Williams, Weymouth, Goodspeed, etc. The Christian whose marriage ends in divorce was not to feel guilty about this, supposing that the unbeliever might have eventually been saved. Paul knew that for some believers to remain in a bad marriage—in a non-spiritual, unbelieving, godless atmosphere—could have a reverse effect, draining the spiritual life of the *believer*.

In Jewish history, as Dr. Edersheim has written, "divorce was *obligatory*...if either party had become heretical, or ceased to profess Judaism." It was not obligatory for a Christian to divorce an unbeliever, but it was certainly permitted when the unbeliever was no longer "pleased" to remain in the marriage. There should be no mistake about this.

LITERAL DEPARTURE ONLY?

"If the unbelieving depart..." We normally think of this only in its primary meaning—a man who literally leaves, moves out of the house, and heads for parts unknown. But is it not also true that some may depart in mind, affection, attitude, and other ways? This kind of "departure" can be just as real, more intense, and worse than the other! Some couples have departed from each other, though they still live under the same roof. In their hearts they are divorced—it just has not been *legally* recorded. Like adultery, a person can depart *in his heart* even though it may not be done literally. There can be little doubt that such departure falls within the spirit of what Paul was saying.

When an Italian man named Caracciolo was converted to Protestantism and fled to Geneva, his wife who was a Catholic refused to go with him. Her refusal indicates a departure in her heart, even though he was the one who literally departed. John Calvin approved of divorce and remarriage for this man under the circumstances. If divorce is inevitable, who actually files for the divorce or who actually departs is really beside the point. If a woman treated a man so bad that she, in effect, drove him off, her claim that *he* "departed" would not make her innocent. The basic point that Paul made was that the Christian was not to be the *cause* of the divorce.

PEACE!

The reason a believer was not bound to an unbeliever who was not "pleased" to remain in a marriage was this: God wants the believer to have *peace*. "Let him depart...*God hath called us to peace."* When Jesus forgave a woman whose sins were "many," he told her to "go in peace" (Luke 7:50). Jesus still wants peace for the believer — including peace in marriage! Such peace was given priority in Paul's program. If a situation becomes such that only through divorce peace can be obtained, then let it be. Divorce was not the original ideal, but neither was marriage if it was unpeaceful. "Can two walk together except they be agreed?" (Amos 3:3). "For where envying and strife is, there is confusion and every evil work" (James 3:16).

If a man is married to a woman with an unbelieving attitude who destroys the harmony of marriage, tears up his Christian literature, causes no end of commotion, and turns the home into a hell, Paul said if she decides to depart to *let her depart.* The man is no longer bound. He might as well say with a sigh

62

"If the unbelieving depart..."
(1 Cor. 7:15)

of relief (as in the song by Roy Clark), "Thank God and Greyhound She's Gone!"

A woman who supposes — contrary to what Paul taught — that God never permits divorce, might refuse a divorce to an unbelieving husband who wants out. He may stay away for months at a time, showing up now and then for a week or so. This is upsetting to the children. There may be the possibility of another pregnancy. It is degrading to the woman to be married — and yet not married. This is not God's plan. The matter should be put to rest — one way or another. "God hath called us to *peace*."

It should be carefully noticed that the reason a Christian was no longer bound to an unbeliever who departed was *not because he was an unbeliever.* It was because there was not *peace!* "Let him depart...but [for, because] God hath called us to peace." The fact that the one who departed was an unbeliever only comes into the picture because his unbelief had disturbed the peace of the marriage. Otherwise, if an unbeliever was "pleased" to remain in the marriage, a believer was not to put him away. The peace of the marriage was the real issue here, divorce being permitted when this peace was no longer present.

Though the lack of peace that Paul dealt with was because a believer was married to an unbeliever, would not the same *principle* apply in other cases? What if both parties are believers, yet they are not "pleased" and there is not "peace"? Just because Paul did not have occasion to deal with this specific situation, does not mean it doesn't exist. In either case, the peace of the marriage is at stake.

63

Even though two people may be good Christians, this does not mean they are good marriage material for each other. I knew a young man who was converted to Christ while in his teens and a short time later married a girl in the church. His decision to marry this particular girl was not because he found her more attractive than other girls he had known, nor was she more compatible, nor did they have much in common. He married her primarily because he thought she was "a good Christian"! A few years later, through much heartache on both sides, the marriage ended in divorce because of insurmountable incompatibility.

Certainly a Christian should marry a Christian. But one does not go out and marry "anyone" just becase he is a Christian! Some might suppose that *any* two Christians should be able to marry and have a good marriage. But if we are honest about it, all of us can probably think right now of many people who are fine Christians, yet we would not want to be married to them! The fact that two people are Christians does not automatically make them compatible marriage partners.

APOSTLES WHO DEPARTED ASUNDER

Even two *apostles* did not always get along with each other. Paul disagreed with Barnabas about including Mark in a preaching trip, "and the *contention* was so sharp between them, that they *departed asunder* one from the other: and so Barnabas took Mark, and sailed unto Cyprus; and Paul chose Silas" (Acts 15:36-40). Had Paul and Barnabas been male and female, they would *not* have been good marriage material for each other — even though both were excellent Christians!

To insist that *all* people who are married stay together in *all* circumstances was not the teaching of Paul. God does not force anyone to get married. Why, then, would he force people to *stay* married when they are not "pleased" with the arrangement and when there is not "peace"? Is a *forced* rela-

64

tionship better for the husband? Is it better for the wife? Some only remain in miserable situations because they are afraid some friend or relative will think evil of them. But each person has a right to his own life. If God has no objection, what business is it of anyone else? Of course a dissolution of marriage should only be considered with utmost caution, realizing that all things that are lawful are not necessarily "expedient" (1 Cor. 6:12) and while we are called unto liberty, we must not use "liberty for an occasion to the flesh" (Gal. 5:13).

Paul was certainly not in the same camp as those who say all remarriage is a sin, as may be seen from the following:

> "Art thou bound unto a wife? seek not to be loosed. Art thou loosed from a wife? seek not a wife. *But and if thou marry, thou hast not sinned;* and if a virgin marry, she hath not sinned" (1 Cor. 7:27, 28).

If a man is "loosed from a wife," there is the implication that he was once "bound" to a wife. A man who has been loosed from a wife does not sin if he remarries — not any more than a virgin (one never married) does by getting married. The reason for this is because marriage is honorable; it was instituted by God.

Some who believe that only death can release a person from the marriage bond, attempt to say the man in this text was "loosed" from marriage because his wife *died.* If being loosed meant his wife had died, what could the expression "seek not to be loosed" mean — that he was seeking her death? This could not be the meaning Paul intended! The word "loosed" in the expression "loosed from a wife" is defined in *Strong's Concordance* (#3080) as "a loosening, i.e. (specifically) *divorce.*"

The words "bound" and "loosed" in the first question and statement present a sharp contrast to each other. If one is bound, he is not loosed; but if he is loosed, he is no longer bound. If no longer bound, it is evident he does not sin by getting married — not even in that "present distress" about which

Paul was concerned for those living at Corinth. This is significant.

THE MARRIAGE CHAPTER

As we seek to understand the over-all teaching of Paul on marriage in this chapter (1 Cor. 7), it is important that we keep in mind the background of the people at Corinth for whom Paul was answering questions. They had been converted as people living in a very immoral city. Some had now gone to the other extreme and supposed that all sexual relations were sinful—*even in marriage*. Some, as Adam Clarke points out, were even teaching the doctrine of "forbidding to marry." In their desire for holy living they had equated sex with sin.

Paul did not want to discourage them in the stand they had taken for holy living, yet it was evident they had exchanged one extreme for another. He agreed only to a certain point, answering that it was "good" for those who were gifted for the single life to be unmarried, pointing out that he was single himself. Otherwise, he explicitly said that "every" person should be married and that sex within marriage was not sinful. Abstinence was to occur only if husband and wife agreed to a temporary time of fasting and prayer (verses 2-5). Paul assured them that becoming a Christian did not require the breakup of marriage. For this he cited the general statement of Jesus, that a man was not to put away his wife (verse 11).

This answered the question for a Christian married to a Christian, but what if a Christian was married to an unbeliever? Apparently they wanted to know if a Christian was defiling himself by having sexual relations with a sinner. Were these acts unholy because the other person was not a believer? Must a Christian put an unbeliever away? Paul assured them that if the unbeliever was pleased to remain in the marriage, the believer was not required to put him or her away. The sexual act was sanctified because of the believer—it was not wrong. Children born to such unions were not unholy (verses 12-14).

66

These answers pertained to those already married. Apparently the Corinthians also wanted to know about those who became Christians who had never been married—virgins. Would it not be more holy for these not to marry? Paul agreed that for some this might be good because of the "present distress," but emphatically pointed out that it was not a sin for a virgin—man or woman—to marry (verses 25, 26).

Some of the Corinthians even questioned if a Christian woman whose husband was dead should remarry—possibly wondering if another sexual relationship for her would be unholy. Paul answered this, quoting a basic point of the law in agreement with his teaching. She was free to marry in the Lord (verse 39).

THE UNMARRIED AND WIDOWS

Having covered all these various situations, one portion of this chapter remains for our attention—that dealing with those who were unmarried and widows. "I say therefore to the *unmarried* and *widows*...if they cannot contain, let them marry: for it is better to marry than to burn [with desire]" (1 Cor. 7:8, 9). When Paul spoke here of the "unmarried," it is doubtful that he meant only those who were "virgins," for he began dealing with that subject in verse 25: "Now concerning virgins..." Probably the "unmarried" included people who had been married before, but who were now single. (The term "unmarried" is used to describe a woman who left her husband in verse 11.) But in what ever circumstances these were single—the "unmarried"—it is clear that celibacy was not required of them. "Let them marry."

Finally, we must notice what Paul said about "widows." This is a point that has been commonly overlooked. As we shall see, Biblically speaking, a widow was simply a woman who had a husband at one time, but did not have one now. Her husband *may* have died, but often she was a widow because

67

he had *deserted* her. (If Paul had meant widows only in the sense of those widowed by death, it would have been unnecessary for him to explain again that a woman whose husband was dead could remarry, as he did clear on down in verse 39.) Because Paul specifically said that widows could remarry, it is important to our present study to show that many widows still had *living* husbands. It is to this point that we now turn special attention.

WIDOWS WITH LIVING HUSBANDS

In modern English, a "widow" is a woman who has lost her husband by death; a "grass widow" is a woman separated from her husband by divorce or absence. But the Bible uses only the one word, "widow," to describe either situation. According to *Strong's Concordance* (#490, the feminine form of #488), the word translated widow in the Old Testament means *"discarded* (as a *divorced* person)."

A woman in 2 Samuel 14:5 said, "I am a widow woman, *and my husband is dead."* If the word "widow" could *only* mean a woman whose husband was dead, for her to add the words "and my husband is dead" would be nonsense. This would be like she said, "I am a woman whose husband is dead, and my husband is dead"! The fact is, either death or desertion could cause a woman to be a widow.

Isaiah, in poetic language, spoke of a woman who married in her "youth," but who was eventually "refused" and "forsaken" by her husband because of barrenness. Nevertheless, she was given this promise: "...thou shalt forget the shame of thy youth, and shalt not remember the reproach of thy *widowhood* any more" (See Isaiah 54:1-10). ("Widowhood" is from the same Hebrew word as "widow.") This woman experienced widowhood, not because her husband died, but because he left her.

Notice how the word "widowhood" is used in 2 Samuel 20:3:

68

"And David came to his house at Jerusalem; and the king took the ten women his concubines...and put them in ward, and fed them, but went not in unto them. So they were shut up unto the day of their death, living in *widowhood*." These women, being separated from their husband David, became widows while David was *still alive*!

When her son died, the widow who had fed Elijah, said, "What have I to do with thee, O thou man of God? art thou come unto me to call my sin to remembrance, and to slay my son?" (1 Kings 17:18). It was a sad situation. Jesus said there were "many widows" in Israel in the days of Elijah (Luke 4:25). Not all of these were widows because the husband had died — many were widows because of desertion.

Over and over the Bible made provision for those who were "fatherless and widows" (Deut. 24:17-21). When harvesting a crop, a portion was to be left for poor people such as these. Anyone even vaguely knowledgeable about the bad economic situation for women in those days can realize why these provisions were made. But if the "fatherless and widows" were only those cases in which the father and husband was *dead*, what about all the other children and wives who needed assistance because the man had *deserted* them? Surely these were included, for the word translated "fatherless" (like that translated "widow") did not necessarily mean the father was dead (*Strong's Concordance*, Old Testament: #3490; New Testament: #3737).

"A sheaf in the field...shall be for...the widow" (Deut. 24:19).

In the New Testament, according to *Strong's Concordance*

(#5503, from #5490), the Greek word translated "widow" means a "*vacancy* through the idea of defficiency; a widow (as *lacking* a husband)," which does not necessarily require the meaning that the former husband had died. Many of these widows had difficulty to survive. The church attempted to help them, such help being termed "pure religion" (see Acts 6:1; 9:41; James 1:27). If only women who were widows by *death* were included in this help, many women who were equally in need would have been excluded—those whose husbands had *deserted* them. All of this is immediately cleared up once we understand the Biblical use of the word widow.

Three classes of widows are distinguished by Paul in 1 Timothy 5: ordinary widows—those without husbands but having some support; widows indeed, those without any support from younger relatives or others; and a group of widows who actually held office as presbyterial widows. These were not to be under sixty years of age. Tertullian, Hermas, and Chrysostom in their writings mention such an order of ecclesiastical widows who ministered to other widows and also to orphans. Paul did not recommend that the younger widows be taken into this particular group, pointing out that they would marry again: "But the younger refuse [for this office]...I will therefore that the young women marry, bear children, guide the house, give none occasion to the adversary to speak reproachfully" (1 Tim. 5:11-14).

Adam Clarke in his note on this portion has commented:

"As the preceding discourse has been about the younger widows, and this is an inference from it; it is most evident that by the *younger women* the apostle means the young *widows*...Here the apostle, so far from forbidding *second* marriages, positively enjoins or at least recommends them. And what man of sense could have done otherwise in the cases he mentions?"[25]

Let me share with you the case of Geraldine who was a "widow" (in my opinion), not because of death, but desertion.

Geraldine's husband, after a few brief years of troubled marriage, deserted her and their two sons, Hal and Ira, who were then ages 2 and 4. He became deeply involved in wild living and drugs. No support was ever sent and the family barely survived. Geraldine was lonely and there was the problem of two boys who would like a father. At this point, she met a very kind and understanding Christian man named Jay. He fell in love with her and was happy with the idea of not only being a husband, but a father to the boys. All concerned were happy with the prospect and Geraldine rejoiced that the Lord was working things out in her life.

Then a clash came with some of the leaders of her church! If she married Jay, she was told, she would be living in adultery. She was told to either return to her husband or remain single the rest of her life. But would going back to a *sinner* be more right than establishing a Christian home with a *believer?* Would taking her children back into a sinful environment be proper for her or them? To remain forever single, was also far from ideal. In this situation, her life for years to come would be that of renting an apartment, living barely above poverty level, and existing from one pay check to another. The boys would grow up without a father and, in her circumstances, would not have steady supervision because she would have to work long hours away from home.

But! if she married Jay, a Christian home could be established. The financial situation would be much better. She would have time to properly care for her sons. She would have the companionship and love of a husband and the boys would have a father. Would it be wrong for Geraldine to take this route? In my opinion, *it would be wrong if she didn't!*

Once we understand the *Biblical* meaning of the word widow, it is clear that Geraldine was just as much a "widow" as if her former husband had died. Not only this, he was "dead in trespasses and sins" (Eph. 2:1), living in sinful "pleasure" made him dead while he yet lived (cf. 1 Tim. 5:6). And whether he was literally dead or not, the *marriage* had obviously died. *The Twentieth Century Encyclopedia of Religious Knowledge* says, "Many spiritually minded pastors believe that adultery or wilful and permanent *desertion* can kill a marriage as surely as though the guilty party were in his grave."[26]

Geraldine's husband had departed, and as Paul said, "Let him depart." Scripturally she was no longer bound to him. Remarriage was her right in the sight of God. As Dr. Hudson has written "...not only does one have the *right* to remarry under some circumstances, it is a *sin* to refrain from remarriage if one's self-fulfillment as a human being can be enhanced by remarriage."[27]

6

LIVING IN ADULTERY?

Jerry and Ann were new Christians. Ann had joined the church as a child but only recently found a vital relationship with God. Jerry had been a kind of rounder, having messed up one marriage, as he stated it. He and Ann had met at a bar. Soon they were married by a justice of the peace. Two years later, with a baby nine months old in the nursery, both Jerry and Ann joined the church. They said they were converted in a Billy Graham crusade. They started reading the Bible for the first time in their lives.

Soon they were in their pastor's study saying, "We don't know what to think. Here in Matthew's Gospel it says that we are *living in adultery,* as we read it. What about this? You know," Jerry said, "I have two children by a former marriage and am paying child support. My X is already married again. But how do we explain this in Matthew 5:32 that says we are living in adultery?"

Here was the pastor's line of reasoning. "In the first place, it does not say anything about *living* in a state of adultery. Adultery is an act. Even if you had been guilty of that when you first married, you were forgiven when you accepted Christ. Second, you can't commit adultery, from a Scriptural point of view, with your own wife or husband. Besides, what kind of a God do you have? It would be crazy to think that he would ask you to give up Ann whom you love, and your baby, and try to go back to your former wife who is already married to somebody else. You were trying to take the Bible seriously. That's great. But taking it seriously is not always the same as taking it literally. Here Jesus was speaking about some very

73

corrupt custom of a man running off his wife after he gave her something written on parchment."

Jerry and Ann began to see that they need not to be hung up on this text, or feel the least inferior about their marriage, that Christian forgiveness turns men and women away from their pasts, and opens up clean uncluttered paths ahead.[28]

INCONSISTENT CONCEPTS

There are couples who have all the fruits of dedicated Christians and whose lives are above reproach — except that one or both of them may have had a previous marriage. Those who believe that only death can sever the marriage bond, cannot accept these people as members of the body of Christ. They must believe these people are just as "lost" as the hardened criminal or pervert! This couple may have been serving the Lord together for fifty years, but as long as a former husband or wife is still living somewhere in this world, they say this couple is "living in adultery"!

This is very inconsistent, for (if correct), salvation for this couple would depend on *when* someone dies! Suppose it was the husband who had a previous marriage. As all people concerned grew older, finally word comes that the man's former wife has died. So, accordingly, the Christian couple (supposedly living in adultery all these years!) is *now* forgiven by God. But what if the man dies *before* his former wife? Then he, according to this reasoning, would be lost simply because *he did not live longer than his former wife!* Or, if he (since *he* was the one married before) dies before his present wife, he "goes to hell" because he was living in adultery when he died. His wife might die *ten minutes later,* but she "goes to heaven" (as they say), for *she* was no longer living in adultery when she died!

I will say here quite simply, God's forgiveness for one individual does not depend on *when* some *other* person dies! The fact is, someone *already* died for all of us: Jesus Christ. "The

74

Lord hath laid on him the iniquity of us all" (Isaiah 53:6). "Christ died for our sins" (1 Cor. 15:3). "He is the propitiation for our sins: and not for ours only, but also for the sins of the whole world" (1 John 2:2). People who have been forgiven of their sins, people who are Christians, are *not* living in adultery.

Evangelist Jimmy Swaggart has summed up the truth on this point in these words:

> The Bible does not use the term "living in adultery" anywhere . . . Those advocating this "doctrine" claim that anyone occupying the marriage bed — where one of the partners had been divorced — is living in a condition of continuing sin. They state that sin is continually being *recommitted,* every time the partners practice marital relations. This does not stand up to scriptural scrutiny. As far as God is concerned, such a couple is living together as husband and wife. Marriage vows have been performed and God *recognizes* them . . . There is nothing in scripture to imply that such a couple will be continuously recommitting the sin of adultery.

> In the circumstances where there were no grounds for divorce . . . there was undeniably a sin committed at the time of divorce. But the sin was a definite entity *at the time of commission,* and was completed within itself. To then harness the person with an ever continuing *succession* of sins, dependent on the first sin, has no basis in scripture.[29]

A person who comes to Christ is not required to break up his present marriage because of a previous marriage (or marriages). The proof of this point may be seen in the experience of those who were converted in Corinth. In a city known for its wickedness and immorality, as the gospel was preached there, *"many* of the Corinthians hearing believed, and were baptized" (Acts 18:8). With hundreds of converts coming into the church, we can be sure that many (if not most!) were not in their "first" marriages. Either the wife had been married before, the husband had been married before — or both of them! — and in this state they were converted. Did the preaching of the gospel demand the breakup of these homes?

No, it did not. There is not the slightest hint of this idea. Instead of being told to break up with their marriage partners, they were told to remain in their marriages if possible (1 Cor. 7:12-14, 20, 27). This included those in first marriages *and those who had been married before.*

If all marital sins and mistakes of the past were not forgiven, Paul would have been *required* to order people — hundreds of them — to divorce and go back to their first mates or, since this would almost always be impossible, to live single the rest of their lives. This he *never* did. It is not that he simply failed to deal with sexual sins, for he gave a strong rebuke about a case of incest at Corinth (1 Cor. 5:1-5). But the normal state of marriage — even though there may have been previous marriages — was upheld. "Let every man abide in the same calling wherein he was called" (1 Cor. 7:20).

"Let not man put asunder" (Matt. 19:6).

When the disciples went forth preaching the gospel, it was not necessary for them to quiz people with all kinds of questions about their past marital history. It was taken for granted that people had sinned. The good news was that God forgives sin and gives people a new start. I have known ministers who were required—contrary to all of this—to interrogate prospective members with very personal and intimate questions, no matter how embarrasing and unfruitful, supposedly to determine if these people could be admitted into "God's true church." Couples with a previous marriage were told they must break up in order to be forgiven. This is a false teaching!

If such breakup was required, the gospel would not be "Believe on the Lord Jesus Christ and thou shalt be saved" (Acts 16:31), but "Believe on the Lord Jesus Christ, and (if remarried), leave your wife and children, live in celibacy, and thou shalt be saved"! No such demand was ever placed on those who came to Christ. People forgiven of their past sins were given a clean slate, they were totally cleansed of past sins, including sexual sins, as the following passage shows:

> "...neither fornicators, nor idolaters, nor *adulterers,* nor effeminate, nor abusers of themselves with mankind, nor thieves, nor covetous, nor drunkards, nor revilers, nor extortioners, shall inherit the kingdom of God. And such *were* some of you: but ye are *washed*, but ye are sanctified, but ye are justified in the name of the Lord Jesus, and by the Spirit of our God" (1 Cor. 6:9-11).

Notice that those who had committed adultery—including those who may have divorced and remarried in an adulterous way—upon being forgiven by Christ were no longer considered adulterers. "Such WERE some of you"—past tense. They were not "living in adultery" (the unscriptural term that some use)! They had been forgiven—they were washed, sanctified, justified! Whatever sins these couples had in their past were forgiven. Those who may have had previous marriages were not given the statis of "second class" Christians—as though God forgives some people more than others.

A CESSPOOL OF SIN

On different occasions I have had the opportunity to speak for a church that has an effective ministry in reaching young people right off the streets and beaches in southern California. Before their conversion, many of these young people were into drugs, occultism, crime, all types of sexual practices, perversion, group sex, homosexuality—a cesspool of sin. It is a beautiful sight to see them clean up, get a job, develop character, settle into marriage—one man and one woman—and establish a Christian home. For any to slice into this with a legalism that would break up this home because of things that happened back in that cesspool of sin, would be self-defeating and evil. Despite whatever mistakes a person may have made in the past, if he gets his life straightened out and goes on from there, this is the important thing. What is past is *forgiven*.

Failure to understand this has caused a lot of unnecessary confusion among some Christians. Take the concern of Kate, a fine Christian woman, for example. One of her sons, Leon, had been quite active as a young person in the church. He married a Christian girl, but the marriage simply did not work out. He later remarried and the second marriage was much more stable. In the hassle though, Leon had dropped out of church. Kate, his mother, found herself in a religious corner. She hoped he would get back into church, but the way they had all been taught, the only way he could "get right with God" would be to break up his home! The whole thing was so depressing and contradictory, she was discouraged from even suggesting his return to church involvement. And Leon, though still a believer in Jesus Christ, lived in condemnation and confusion.

I believe the Holy Spirit will use this book, *Divorce and Remarriage—What Does the Bible Really Say?*, to help people in situations such as this. The strict, unforgiving, inflexible attitude that some have developed concerning divorce and

78

remarriage does harm to the work of God, as the following example shows.

In a church that was growing and glowing for Christ — doing a good work in the community it served — someone decided to make an issue about divorce and remarriage. One man, especially, felt this was his "calling." It so happened that a man in the church who had a previous marriage (and had since remarried) was the teacher of the Bible class for the young people. He did an excellent job and had the respect of the young people. (He believed God had forgiven him for the mistake he had made in marriage years before.) The man in the church who was making an issue of this situation had a son in this man's class and let it be known he would not have an "adulterer" teaching his son!

People began to take sides. The root of bitterness grew. The man was asked to resign as teacher. A number of young people felt (and understandably so) that the whole thing was ridiculous. There were many hurts. Finally the church split and dwindled down to almost nothing. Of course the few who were left probably felt confident they were "right," but the church never regained its effectiveness in the community.

When the people of this church were confronted with the possibilities of what could happen, they had to decide what was most important to them. In order to be "scriptural" (supposedly) on one point, they caused a whole string of *unscriptural* things. They sacrificed, as it were, their young people and the outreach of the church in that community. In choosing their priorities, they exalted principles above people. If God has forgiven a person, who are we to act as judges and say he has not? With Paul I say:

"Why dost thou judge thy brother? or why dost thou set at nought thy brother? for we shall all stand before the judgment seat of Christ...I am persuaded by the Lord Jesus, that there is nothing unclean of itself...Destroy not him for whom Christ died...Let us therefore follow after the things which make for peace, and things wherewith one may edify another...Destroy not the work of God" (Rom. 14:10-20).

FIRST MARRIAGES

Those who say God only recognizes "first" marriages, claim that a man who remarries is not a husband, he is an "adulterer." This is not the *scriptural* position. Jesus told the woman at

"Thou hast had five husbands" (John 4:18).

Jacob's well, "...thou has had *five* husbands; and he whom thou now hast is not thy husband" (John 4:18). The point is, she had been married five times and each man in succession was her "husband," not just the first. The man she was now living with, but not actually married to, was *not* her husband. Jesus did not say the four men she married after the "first" were not husbands. No, she had had five husbands. The idea that only the first man she married was her "husband," and all after that were simply "adulterers," is not the Biblical terminology.

According to the terminology used in the Bible, after a woman is divorced "she may go and be another man's *wife*. And if the latter *husband* [the second husband] hate her...or die...her *former husband*, which sent her away, may not take her again to be his wife" (Deut. 24:1-4). Her second marriage involved a "husband" and she was a "wife." The first man she was married to is then spoken of as her *"former* husband." If she was still married to the first husband "in the sight of

80

God" (as some say), when she married again, such would not only have been adultery, it would have been bigamy! Since her "former husband" was never to take her again to be his wife, it is obvious she was *not* still married to him in the sight of God.

The idea that God recognizes only *first* marriages is not only unscriptural, it is inconsistent with itself, as the following example about Lucy will show.

Lucy married Marvin at age 18 after they went together for a short time. Both were nominal Christians, but very young and immature. The marriage lasted only two years and ended in divorce. Lucy later married Neal who had not been married before. Children were born. About fifteen years later, they were confronted with the teaching that God only recognizes "first" marriages. Since this was her second marriage, they were told they were not truly married "in the sight of God," that they were "living in adultery." This resulted in a lot of unrest and confusion. Lucy became interested in another man, and when word came that Marvin, husband number 1, had died suddenly, she left Neal for this other man who became husband number 3. *If* God does not recognize a second marriage, she was totally free to do this!

Her first husband died — she could not go back to him. Her second marriage, according to the belief, was not recognized by God. So leaving this was not wrong — she was only quitting a life of adultery! — and was free to marry a third time since her *only* "husband" was now dead! To go a step further, according to this idea, suppose she had married six times. If only the "first" marriage was recognized by God, just as soon as husband number 1 died, she could marry the *seventh* time! It is ridiculous, yet this is typical of the problems the legalists make for themselves.

No wonder Swaggert has written: "There is a 'teaching' which states that the *first* person married by someone is forever after recognized by God as his partner, and any subsequent marriage is *not* recognized by God. This is *patently untrue.*"³⁰

HUSBAND OF ONE WIFE

Those who believe God only recognizes "first" marriages sometimes quote 1 Timothy 3:2: "A bishop must be...the husband of *one* wife." They take this to mean God only allows one marriage and in this case, specifically, a man who has remarried after divorce cannot be a minister. This is not the point at all. A minister was to have one wife — *one wife at the time.* If this is not the correct meaning, then even a man whose wife *died* could not be a minister if he remarried. If Paul means a minister was permitted only one *marriage* in life, he could have used a very common Greek word to describe this. He could have said, "...married [*gameo*] only once." But he used a different construction altogether.

A bishop was to be "the husband of one wife." A man with a previous marriage which ended because of death or divorce — and who was now "the husband of one wife" — met the qualification laid down by Paul. If he was now "the husband of two or three wives," he did *not*. Though the practice of polygamy was not actually unscriptural, a turning away from this impractical custom had developed by this time, and the minister was to set an example by following this trend. The requirement was not on moral grounds, but practical.

I can honestly say that some of the finest, most dedicated Christians I have known, have been people who experienced failure in marriage at some point in the past and who, subsequently, have remarried. Because they have remarried is no sign they lack devotion. Many of these would become *martyrs* — if need be — for Christ himself. They just do not believe they were meant to be martyrs for a meaningless marriage. If God has forgiven people of their past marital mistakes or sins — if *he* has accepted them — why shouldn't we?

How often did Jesus tell us to forgive others? Seven times a day? No, Jesus spoke of "seventy times seven" (Matt. 18:22). Some who read these words of Jesus fail to comprehend, apparently, that Jesus is just that willing to forgive. If he is not, why did he tell others to do something he himself would not do? He not only forgives our sins, he forgets them! (Heb. 10:17).

The Bible does not condemn all cases of divorce — obviously (Gen. 21:10-14; Deut. 24:1-4; Ezra 10:3; Jer. 3:8; Matt. 19:9; 1 Cor. 7:15). But *even if it did* — and if it condemned divorce as sin from Genesis to Revelation! — all preaching against divorce would be totally *unbalanced* if the message did not include the fact that GOD FORGIVES SIN. There are some preachers who take a hard stand against people who have made marital mistakes, yet some of these have a problem with lust in their own minds and hearts. In a quarter of a century in the ministry now, I have known literally hundreds of ministers in various denominations. Not one of them is perfect. And while some do not have marital troubles — so far as I might know — not one is in a position to throw any stones. People with a previous marriage have often faced enough difficulties in life without the preacher giving them a black eye every time they go to church.

A HOUSE CLEANING?

A preacher who was ready to "clean house," as he put it, declared that no person in his church who had a previous marriage could sing in the choir, hold any position in the church, or even serve as an usher! "I don't believe in second marriages!" he said. A close friend of his (who had divorced and remarried) said to him in private, "I know you have only married once, but did you ever have a sexual relationship with another woman?" (Being close friends, neither considered this conversation too personal.) With some hesitation the pastor admitted there had been some involvement with a prostitute when he was in Vietnam in the service. Then, too, there was an incident with a woman when he was a teen-ager — a woman who did baby sitting for his younger brother and sister in the home. But there were only these two women before he married his wife. "Well," the other man replied, "you have been married to *three* women and never even divorced the first two. I have been married only twice, but *I* got a divorce!"

Some might feel this is not a fair comparison because the pastor had not *legally* married the prostitute or the baby sitter. But, *Biblically* speaking, is there really that much difference? Within marriage two people become "one," Jesus pointed out, quoting Genesis 2:24. Paul taught that a man who has sexual relations with a harlot also becomes "one," and quoted the *same* verse! "Know ye not that he which is joined to an harlot is one body? for two, saith he, shall be one flesh" (1 Cor. 6:16).

You see, our idea of a marriage — with a minister performing a ceremony — was not the custom in Bible times. It is not improper, of course, for a minister to do this, but we just never read of Peter or Paul doing it. That was not the custom then. Back then, an agreement may have been made between heads of families — a gift or bride price may have changed hands — but it was through sexual union that a couple was considered "one." It was when Isaac took Rebekah into the tent, for example, that "she became his wife" (Gen. 24:67).

In view of these things, men who have been involved sexually with other women prior to marriage, but who boast their is a "first" marriage — and possibly condemn those in a "second" marriage — are really not so righteous and holy as they profess.

SAVED FROM SIN!

Some months ago I heard a man give his testimony about how God saved him from a very wicked life. Though raised in church, he had rebelled at an early age, became involved with gangs, got into drugs, cursed God, chased women — living with one and then another — though he never "legally" married. Then he got saved, went to Bible school where he married a Christian girl, and is now an ordained minister. We can all rejoice in what God has done for him. But there is a serious *inconsistency* here. The denomination which ordained him does not allow divorce and remarriage. Had he married even *one* of these women he lived with, any marriage after that would not be "first" marriage and ordination would have been refused!

If this man who lived in sin with *many* women was allowed to marry, why shouldn't a man who married *one* woman have the same right? Assuming both men were unsaved at the time, the only difference between the two would be that one had a piece of paper (a marriage certificate) and the other did not! Is God's power to give a man a clean slate limited by a piece of paper? The one man may have lived with a hundred women — and even fathered children for all he knew or cared at the time. When he received Christ, he was allowed to marry, most pastors would have gladly officiated at his wedding, and he was ordained to the ministry.

But the other man who had the decency to actually marry a woman (but whose marriage ended in divorce), when he receives Christ, marriage for him is frowned on. If he remarries it is "living in adultery," the way some look at it. Some ministers would not be allowed to perform a ceremony for him. Any other sin he might have committed could be wiped out as though it had never been, but with a previous marriage, according to some, he must atone for this by staying single the rest of his life!

The inconsistency of this double standard says, in effect, 'Don't get married — just live with different ones. God will forgive this, and if you do finally get married it will be a *first* marriage. But if you marry and it doesn't work out, you can never get married again. God won't forgive this because he does not accept *second* marriages." How silly can some get?

THE CAR THIEF

"But," some object, "a couple in a second marriage must break up in order for God to forgive them just like a man who steals a car must return it!" We agree that a man who took a car should not keep driving around in a stolen car. He should return it to the rightful owner — *if he can!* But in many cases he can not. It may have been years before that the crime was committed. He may not even know who the car belonged to. The former owner may have already collected insurance. He may be dead. Does this man who took a car remain forever unforgiven because circumstances will not permit a return? In such complex situations, God simply forgives a repentant heart and gives the man a clean slate.

Besides, the return of a car and the return of a wife, as it were, do not provide a valid comparison. A car is a thing, not a person. A car does not love, does not have emotions, does not think, does not involve children. Did the man who is remarried actually steal the woman? Did he take her against her will? Was not the marriage by mutual agreement? The concept of returning stolen property could seldom apply here.

For people in second marriages to return to their first mates is, in the vast majority of cases, impossible. God does not require the impossible. He simply forgives and that's that. According to Deuteronomy 24:4, at least, once one had actually remarried, there was to be no return to the previous mate, ever if the second husband died. Only in a very unique situation might it be otherwise (cf. Jer. 3:1).

Some teach that if it is impossible to go back to a first hus band or wife, then a person must live single. But celibacy i not God's plan. Suppose a car thief repents and tries to return a stolen car. He cannot find the owner. He feels it would be wrong for him to keep the car. So he takes it and *pushes it over a cliff!* The car is destroyed; no one has the benefit of it. As silly as this is, this is the "logic" of those who insist that people with previous marriages must separate and remain single. Who benefits? A woman does not have a husband, a husband does not have a wife, children do not have their parents, their economic situation suffers, two residences must be maintained, etc. Such is legalism — that one should push his happiness, his effectiveness, his peace of mind, his marriage, over a cliff — all because of an interpretation some have forced on a very tiny portion of scripture!

RESTITUTION?

Suppose an elderly man who was once wealthy receives Christ in his latter years. He has lost his fortune and is now poor. All those years he did not support the work of God. Now he has come to Christ and asked for forgiveness. Must he somehow pay back money for all those years he "robbed God" in order to be forgiven? No! His case would be like that described in Luke 7:41, 42: "There was a certain creditor which had two debtors: the one owed five hundred pence, and the other fifty. And when they had nothing to pay, he frankly forgave them both." Some mistakes or sins of the past simply cannot be made right. When people have made a mess of their married life, God just frankly forgives!

A man who commits murder cannot bring his victim back from the dead, yet he can be forgiven. Moses, the very one who gave the commandment "Thou shalt not kill," had once killed a man (Exodus 2:12). He was forgiven and used of God in a tremendous way after that. It is a very limited view of the grace of God to suppose that only things that can be made "right" can be forgiven.

87

It is strange to me that people can believe murder is forgiven—even though the situation is not reversed—but a second marriage cannot be forgiven unless people break up? This inconsistency brings to mind something a minister shared with me some years ago. His wife had divorced him for what she felt was incompatibility. Some years later he remarried. There were those who felt he had sinned in getting married a "second" time. "I could have taken a gun and *killed* my first wife," he told me. "I might have gone to prison for a while, but they believe God could forgive me for murder. With her dead, and me forgiven, I could *then* remarry with the blessing of my demonination!"

In the Bible, David had Bathsheba's husband killed and then married her. Was he forgiven for this? As bad and irreversible as this sin was, he was forgiven. Question! Can a man who marries a divorced woman, but who does *not* kill her former husband, be forgiven? The answer is so obvious we wonder why people have stumbled over it.

WHAT ABOUT CHRISTIANS WHO DIVORCE AND REMARRY?

In the case of Jerry and Ann (p. 73), divorce and remarriage had taken place *before* they were converted. God gave them a clean slate. But what about those who are already Christians who divorce and remarry, possibly without valid grounds? Can they be forgiven? This answer is, of course, yes. "Christians," a bumper sticker says, "are not perfect—just forgiven!" I might add that they are not just part way forgiven—they are perfectly forgiven. "The blood of Jesus Christ...cleanseth us from *all* sin" (1 John 1:7). If we sin, forgiveness is available. Notice what the Bible says about Christians and the forgiveness of sin:

"If *we* [Christians] say that we have no sin, we deceive ourselves...if we confess our sins, he is faithful and just to forgive us *our* sins...and

88

if any man sin, we have an advocate with the Father, Jesus Christ the righteous: and he is the propitiation [atoning sacrifice] for *our* sins: and not for ours only, but also for the sins of the whole world" (1 John 1:8-2:2).

Forgiveness for sin is found in Jesus Christ — not only for the sins of the unconverted world — but for "our sins" *as believers!* The concept that God forgives the sinner one time — when he is drawn to Christ — and forgiveness stops there, is neither realistic or scriptural. If a believer sins, he has an advocate and friend in Jesus. It is very inconsistent to suppose that God would forgive harlots, playboys, swingers, and sex perverts who repent of their sins, but would not forgive mistakes and sins of his own children! Quoting again from Swaggart:

> What about Christians who divorce without grounds, and then remarry?...Can these divorced people be forgiven by God and cleansed of their sin? *Of course they can.* Some might ask, "If people precipitate such a course of events, *knowing* what they are doing and the consequences of it, surely they can never be forgiven." Well, anyone holding such a position is making laws, rather than reading the ones God made..."But wait," you say, "this opens an easy path. All anyone has to do is divorce, remarry, ask God's forgiveness, and then everything is all right. Why, one could do this over and over again." Yes, in all honesty he could, if he had a truly repentant heart after each occurance. That's what God's grace and mercy are all about. But in practice, how many people would *want* to set off on such a round of problems?"[31]

It should be pointed out that in taking this stand, Swaggart was not speaking from convenience, but conviction, for his denomination does not officially permit any divorce and remarriage.

A SECOND DIVORCE?

Must a *Christian* who divorces and remarries — possibly without totally valid grounds — break up his marriage in order for God to forgive him? No. Two wrongs do not make a right. Bible believers will want some Biblical principle, of course, by which to establish this conclusion, and that we will give.

We are told in the Bible that a Christian is to marry "only in the Lord" (1 Cor. 7:39) and is not to be "unequally yoked together with unbelievers" (2 Cor. 6:14). However, it does happen, does it not? The believer who has married an unbeliever has gone against the Bible—has committted sin. Is the believer forgiven this sin without breaking up the home? Certainly. Remember Paul's words about a believer married to an unbeliever:

> "If any brother hath a wife that believeth not, and she be pleased to dwell with him, let him not put her away. And the woman which hath an husband that believeth not, and if he be pleased to dwell with her, let her not leave him" (1 Cor. 7:12, 13).

A believer who repents for marrying an unbeliever is forgiven *without breaking up his marriage.* On this same basis, if a believer committed sin when he divorced and remarried, this is also forgiven without tearing apart another marriage.

OTIS AND PEARL

If God forgives the *sins* of sinners, surely he does not hold an honest *mistake* against one of his own children. Some people that Otis knew were not so sure about this! See what you think.

Otis and Pearl—both Christians—had been married for 30 years. They were both the same age, had married at 20 and now, at age 50, Pearl suddenly died. All these years she had been a housewife while Otis pursued his job. Otis felt lost without her. After a few months passed, he began to see a neighbor woman whose husband had died a few years before. Soon they married, but it did not work out. They were incompatible, there were problems involving her children by the previous marriage, and after a few months they parted as friends. Both realized they had rushed into something too quickly.

A year passed and Otis had time to weigh things. He met a woman with whom he was very compatible, with many of the same likes and dislikes as his own. After going together for a period of time, they married. They were very happy together, but then the religious problem came up. Some held it against him because, as they put it, he had a former "living" wife! The fact that the other marriage was brief, was done in loneliness on the rebound, and involved circumstances that were unknown to him at the time, seemed to matter little to the legalists. He had transgressed their taboo and they felt he could no longer be in fellowship with God or the church.

People who have no better understanding of the scriptures than this may claim to be super Christians, filled with the Holy Spirit and faith; but they actually have a deficient faith concerning God's grace. They do err, not knowing the scriptures or the power of God.

"The forgiveness principle," writes Pastor Bob Brown, "is the great theme of the Bible. The theme of redemption, beginning again, is also a primary Biblical thrust. The *ideals* are clearly set out in the Scriptures, but when we fall short of the ideal, *we can start over*. Because love and marriage are so important, I think that *especially* the divorced person can start over. Or what is Christianity about?"[32] There is, after all, forgiveness for failure, mercy for mistakes, and salvation for sin!

We should not forget that in the Bible there were very strong believers who at times committed great sins and were forgiven. The sin of David cannot be excused as a sin committed before he knew God. His marriage to Bathsheba was sinful—he didn't repent until after the marriage—*yet he was forgiven*. The pro-

"David the king said unto all the congregation, Solomon my son, whom God hath chosen" (1 Chron. 29:1).

phet of God rebuked him for his sin, but he was not told to break up his marriage. Because the sin was forgiven, even *this* marriage was recognized by God as valid and was blessed. It was from this union that Solomon was born, who was "beloved of his God" (Neh. 13:26). He was chosen to sit in "the throne of the Lord" over Israel and of him it was said there was none wiser (1 Chron. 29:23; 1 Kings 4:31). It was through this lineage (involving David and Bathsheba) that Jesus himself came who was, like Solomon, called the son of David (Matt. 1:1).

Interestingly enough, in the genealogy of Christ recorded in Matthew, of the four women mentioned—Tamar, Rahab, Ruth, and Bathsheba—three are linked in Biblical history with immorality! One was an adulteress and two had been prostitutes. Why would these women be expressly mentioned in the genealogy of Christ? Is it not possible that even this illustrates the fact that God forgives sin?

Knowing the greatness of God's forgiveness could inspire David with words such as those found in Psalm 103:1-17:

"The Lord is merciful and gracious, slow to anger, and plenteous in mercy. He will not always chide: neither will he keep his anger for ever. He hath not dealt with us after our sins: nor rewarded us according to our iniquities. For as the heaven is high above the earth, so great is his mercy toward them that fear him. As far as the east is from the west, so far hath he removed our transgressions from us. Like as a father pitieth his children, so the Lord pitieth them that fear him. For he knoweth our frame; he remembereth that we are dust...the mercy of the Lord is from everlasting to everlasting."

I am very well aware of the scripture that says we are not to continue in sin that *grace* may abound (Rom. 6:1); and I know, also, that men might try to misuse the idea of *grace* as an excuse to do wrong. Nevertheless, try as we may, none can fully measure up to the high standards of a perfect God. Any and all who have ever been saved, have been saved through the *grace* of God. "For by *grace* are ye saved through faith; and that not of yourselves: it is the *gift* of God: not of works, lest any man should boast" (Eph. 2:8).

It is this grace that could inspire a hymn writer (Julia H. Johnston, 1849-1919) with these words:

"Grace, grace, God's grace, grace that will pardon and cleanse within; grace, grace, God's grace, *grace that is greater than all our sin!*"

The greatness of God's grace could cause Charles Wesley (1707-1788) to write a hymn with these words:

"O for a thousand tongues to sing my great Redeemer's praise!
The glories of my God and King, the triumphs of his *grace*.
He breaks the power of canceled *sin*, he sets the prisoner *free*;
His blood can make the *foulest* clean; *his blood availed for me.*"

To believe that the grace of Christ is greater than all our sin is not to *minimize* sin; instead it *magnifies* Christ and his power to forgive!

7

STRAINING AT A GNAT

Many years ago a missionary who had spent most of his life on the foreign field was returning home. On the ship, when served ice cream for the first time in his life, he exclaimed, "Eating ice cream *must* be a SIN—it tastes *so good*!"

This incident, though quite simplistic, reflects a concept that many of us grew up with. If we had to choose between two viewpoints—one very strict and the other not so strict—we would automatically assume that *God required the strict way.* This is not necessarily true. The strict people would have stoned to death the woman taken in adultery, but this was not the attitude of Jesus. Even though they could quote "scripture" for their position, it was evident they had allowed law to supersede love. This same strictness caused some to want to *kill* Jesus because he had healed on the sabbath! (John 8:5; 5:16).

According to the strict people, it was not appropriate for Jesus, being a religious teacher among the Jews, to converse with a woman in a public place as he did at Jacob's well. Besides, this woman was a Samaritan, had been married five times, and was now living with a man she was not married to! Even the disciples "marvelled that he talked with the woman" (John 4:7-27).

How shocked the strict people must have been when Jesus said: "The *harlots* go into the kingdom before you"! (Matt. 21:31). But repentance comes easier to sinners than to self-righteous people who feel they have no need of repentance. Jesus was criticized for eating and drinking with sinners; but, as he pointed out, these were the ones he came to help (Mark

2:16, 17). Some people still have problems understanding why Jesus turned water into wine at a wedding festival in Cana (John 2:9). The attitude of Jesus was not the strict, holier-than-thou attitude. He was not a compromiser—not by any means—he just did not major on minors.

People who become so strict on one thing, often do so at the expense of other things which may be more important. Jesus said they "strain at a gnat [or literally, strain out a gnat], and swallow a camel." In their strictness for the letter of the law, they would strain water or wine through linen gauze lest a tiny insect be swallowed; yet they would turn right around and swallow a camel, as it were, neglecting matters of greater importance such as judgment, mercy, and faith! (Matt. 23:23, 24).

"Hypocrites...which strain at a gnat, and swallow a camel" (Matt. 23:23, 24).

Being strict just for the sake of being strict is unfruitful. "Why tempt ye God," Peter said, "to put a yoke upon the neck of the disciples, which neither our fathers nor we were able to bear?" (Acts 15:10). A study of Acts 15 shows that the apostles were against imposing rules on people that God has not placed on them. This was no lowering of standards nor did it indicate any spiritual laxness on their part. Jesus spoke

"Burdens...grievous to be borne" (Matt. 23:4).

of those who make unnecessary religious requirements in these words: "They bind heavy burdens and grievous to be borne, and lay them on men's shoulders; but they themselves will not move them with one of their fingers" (Matt. 23:4).

St. Pachomius for fifty years never laid down while sleeping. Marcarius slept in a marsh for six months exposing his naked body to poisonous flies. Simeon of Syria built a column sixty feet high on which he lived for thirty years exposed to rain, sun, and cold. In a convent of the fourth century, 130 nuns never bathed or washed their feet. St. Marcian restricted himself to one meal a day in order to be continually plagued with hunger. Did any of this strictness make these people more holy?

There have been monks who have gone for years without uttering a word. Did this make them victorious and effective witnesses for Christ? There have been men who lived in monasteries or deserted places so they would not see the face of a woman. Yet, many were like St. Jerome who confessed: "When I was living in the desert...how often did I fancy myself among the pleasures of Rome!...I often found myself amid bevies of girls. My face was pale and my frame chilled with fasting; yet my mind was burning with desire, and the fires of lust kept bubbling up." Some became so strict they even castrated themselves, a notable example being Origen.

The strict teaching about divorce and remarriage has caused many people to feel they are eternally trapped in a miserable marriage or doomed to celibacy the rest of their lives. This strictness is not Biblical, it does not reflect the total attitude of Jesus, and does a lot of unnecessary harm.

There are countless women who have been married to wife beaters, have endured insults, indignities, and cruelties from fiendish husbands, supposing they must stay in this situation to do "the will of God"! The idea that every Christian must stay in a bad marriage—"no matter what"—forces people onto a fruitless, dead end street.

Take Rhoda for example. After about two years of marriage, it became very evident that a serious mistake had been made. Her husband's concept of a wife, come to find out, was that of a drudging slave or cheap substitute for a prostitute. It was not uncommon for him to come home in a drunken condition and demand "love." He was obnoxious in actions and cleanliness. Virtues such as loving, caring, sharing, and trust were no longer present in the marriage. There was strife, confusion, and unhappiness. Rhoda questioned whether it would even be *right* to bring children into this "home."

According to the strict people, Rhoda must stay in this

 miserable marriage and bring children into this misery also! Imagine that. No matter how mismatched, no matter how miserable, no matter how unhappy, there are actually people who suppose God would never permit an end to this self-defeating arrangement. A mistake was made and must be continually perpetuated so that it automatically leads to thousands of mistakes through an entire lifetime!

"Let all bitterness, and wrath, and anger, and clamor...be put away from you" (Eph. 4:31).

This concept has so pressured people that some have actually wished their husband or wife would *die,* so they could remarry and remain within the grace of God. On three or four occasions, I have actually had people tell me they have *prayed* for the death of the other person. They were not proud of this; they were perplexed by it.

UNTIL DEATH?

Many suppose the words "until death do you part" or "as long as you both shall live" are in the Bible. They are not. Of course these words, commonly used in wedding ceremonies, do express a beautiful ideal. One should never approach the marriage altar with intentions for anything less than a lifelong relationship. In the reality of life, however, even people with all good intentions have "parted" because of death—not the death of the individuals concerned—but the *marriage itself has died.*

It does not take literal death to terminate a marriage. On numerous occasions the Bible speaks of death in ways other than literal death, as when it says, "She that liveth in pleasure is *dead while she liveth"* (1 Tim. 5:6). In some cases, the death of marriage comes quickly, as in cases of immorality. In other cases, it results from a combination of things. The cup finally becomes full and overflows. But whether it comes instantly, or because of prolonged illness and various complications, the final result is the same: marital death.

Pride may cause some to pretend it has not happened. Some may continue in a marital masquerade to preserve an image of faithfulness or legal unity. They may still live under the same roof and go through the marital ritual, yet if *love* is not present, the *life* of marriage is gone. If a marriage has breathed its last breath, there is no need for two people to accuse each other or to seek vengeance. Since neither person is perfect, since there is some blame on both sides, why not just admit it and

99

be done with it? If all attempts to restore a dead marriage to life have failed, as unpleasant as it may be, a person might just as well go ahead and make the funeral arrangements.

Dr. William Barclay has pointed out that "there are other things than adultery which can *kill* a marriage and the love which should be in it." He recommends that two married people who find themselves in an impossible situation seek counseling and try to work things out. If, however, the situation is still beyond mending,

> "...then I do not think that it is an act of Christian love to keep two such people tied together in a life of torture; nor do I think that it is right for them to be allowed to separate and never be allowed to try to start again. In such circumstances I believe that divorce is the action of Christian love, for I do not think that Jesus would have insisted that two utterly incompatible people should be condemned to drag out a loveless existence, heartbreaking for themselves and disastrous for their children. Nor do I believe that they should be forbidden to remarry and to remarry with the blessing of the church. Nor do I think I would wish to talk much about innocent and not innocent parties, for when marriage breaks up I should doubt if there is any such thing as an altogether innocent and an altogether guilty party."[33]

SECOND-CLASS CHRISTIANS?

There has been a lot of inconsistency on the part of preachers who claim to oppose all divorce and remarriage. They may take a remarried couple into the fellowship of the local church, but they would not perform a wedding ceremony for that couple! They might allow them to be members, but will not allow them to hold any office in the church. By these actions, are they not saying, in effect, that God has forgiven some people *more* than others? If sinners (with one marriage) can be saved and serve, why can't a sinner (with a previous marriage) be *just as saved* and able to *serve*? Some preachers will not totally accept the marriage of a couple who has remarried, yet they will accept their money! I say, if they cannot accept their *marriage,* they should not accept their *money.*

Some who preach against divorce, pointing out the problems of broken homes, should be consistent and also point out problems in homes that are *not* broken. They talk about problems in "second" marriages, as though there were no problems in "first" marriages! Some attempt to show that second marriages are never as good as first marriages — that second marriages labor under the curse of unhappiness. This is certainly not always the case, as the following letter shows:

Dear Pastor Woodrow,...At age three my father left my mother and moved to another state. There were two children, my brother and myself. He was two years older and had just started school. Though I was a very young girl at the time, I can still recall times of anger between my parents, loud yelling, threats, etc. When my father left, we did not know where he was for quite a few years and, perhaps needless to say, he sent no support for us or help with the rent. It was quite a struggle. A couple years later, my mother met a fine Christian man, kind and good, whom she married. Sure it was her "second marriage" which the church we attended considered a sin. But where was the sin? Who was being harmed? This man provided for us, raised us, loved us as though we were his own and, as far as I'm concerned, he *is* my father! His marriage to mom brought a security, a peace, a happy childhood for me in those years of growing up. The arguing and fighting I had remembered from the other marriage were, thank God, only haunting memories of the past. Though some of the church people continued to believe mom's "second marriage" was a sin, to us *it was the answer to our prayers!*

GRATEFUL IN GLENDALE.

The way some look at it, each person is given only *one* chance in life at marriage. If he makes a mistake with that one chance, he must be penalized forever after! If this is true, how can we explain the fact that there are literally thousands and thousands of dedicated Christian couples who have had a previous marriage? "Let me say quite frankly that in some cases where a first marriage has ended in tragedy," writes Geoffrey F. Fisher, Archbishop of Canterbury, "a second marriage has, by every test of the presence of the Holy Spirit that we are able to recognize, been abundantly *blessed*. For this very reason I do not find myself able to *forbid* good people who come to me for advice to embark on a second marriage."[34]

IRRECONCILABLE DIFFERENCES

There was a time when people felt courts must hear all the details about why two people wanted to dissolve their marriage. States which adopted an "irreconcilable differences" clause simplified the whole thing. Instead of courts being hopelessly backed up by hearing all kinds of dirt and gossip, more time could be utilized in forming a legal settlement for the parties concerned. Christians would be wise if they could recognize the bulk of Christian divorce cases as just this: the people concerned had irreconcilable differences and whatever details entered into this are the business of those concerned. Each will answer to God. For fellow Christians to allow themselves to become nosy is inexcusable.

Some things are better left untold. A pastor of a large church was involved in a divorce. His church board told him that if his wife had committed adultery, he could remain as pastor. Otherwise, they were asking for his resignation. There were children involved and, out of a heart of concern, he would not tell them she had indeed committed adultery. To tell the board members details of her infidelty would have only leaked the whole thing to the church and community. These men who asked for his resignation could not possibly know the intimate problems with which the marriage was entangled — nor was it any of their business! It is not hypocrisy for a person to remain silent about some things.

I knew a young minister who was pastoring a small church and the only piano player was his wife. If everything did not go to suit her, she would not go to church and play the piano. Her absence was, of course, very noticeable! When people asked him why she was not there, he attempted to give evasive answers, not wanting to discourage anyone by explaining the real reason. "If I leave you," she would threaten, "you won't survive in the ministry." Their denominational policy did not permit divorce! Though she had some good points, she seemed to be driven with an inner need to control others, especially him. He put up with a lot of unpleasant things because of his desire to continue in the work of God. He once shared something with me that was very intimate: sometimes he felt that sexual contact with her was almost *adultery*. They were not together on so many other things, getting together sexually seemed hypocritical. Eventually the marriage did end in divorce.

DEDICATION AND DIVORCE

As strange as it may sound to some, a divorce may be the very sign of one's dedication to God! It was for Scott, a young Bible school student whose wife left him. She filed for divorce simply because she refused to be a preacher's wife. He loved her dearly, but through much prayer and soul searching was willing to give her up because of God's call on his life. Because of the divorce, the vast majority of churches in his denomination would not think of calling him to be their pastor. Yet, the divorce was clearly a sign of his dedication. Though he was a capable preacher, at last count the only position he held in the church was that of a janitor! What a waste.

There are always those who suggest that if there is enough dedication to God, enough faith, enough patience, enough forgiveness, a person will *always* be able to work out *all* marital difficulties. This is simply *not* true. The Lord himself did not solve all the problems he had with the wife he had chosen! Repeatedly this was the theme of the prophets (Ezekiel 16; Jeremiah 3; Isaiah 50). Would any say *he* did not have enough dedication, enough faith, enough patience, enough forgiveness? Even very fine ministers are not exempt from problems, sometimes problems within marriage. We should not write off men of God who after years of strife and perplexing problems have finally divorced.

Church people who have the attitude that they want nothing to do with people who have gone through a divorce are not very consistent. They fail to consider that in their relationship with GOD, they are dealing with a *divorced person!* (Jer. 3:8). Sometimes a Christian who is involved in a divorce may feel he is a *failure.* This is *not* true. Was the Lord a failure when he went through a divorce? Divorce should not be equated with doom or disaster.

Some people actually mature spiritually after going through a divorce. They may realize they had judged, criticized, and condemned others who had experienced a marital breakdown. Only after going through a divorce themselves — perhaps even the type that needed forgiveness — did they realize the truth contained in the words of Jesus, "To whom little is forgiven, the same loveth little" (see Luke 7:47).

On several occasions, Jesus spoke out against the falseness of those who "trusted in themselves that they were righteous, and despised others." He told of two men who went up to the temple to pray. The one was a Pharisee — a member of the "holiness" branch of the Jewish religion — and how proud he was! Even in his prayer he boasted of how he was not as other men — "adulterers," etc. But the prayer of the other man — who realized he was a *sinner* — carried more weight with God than that of the self-righteous Pharisee (Luke 18:9-11).

Our English word "adultery" comes from the same word as "ulterior." If a person says one thing but intends another, we say he has an ulterior motive. He adds *ulter* to the situation. Sexually speaking, this *ad-ulter-y* forms our word adultery. If people divorce and remarry in an adulterous way, it is ulterior, wrong, and sinful — but it should not be treated as an unpardonable sin. It should not be looked on as a sin that is *more difficult* for God to forgive than other sins!

SECOND THOUGHTS

I suppose every Christian writer who puts out a book on divorce and remarriage has some second thoughts. Hudson says those who write on this subject will be "shot at." He admits he is gun-shy and points out that "religious people can be very malicious as well as very understanding and tolerant." Whatever position a person takes, he opens himself up to a lot of criticism and possible misunderstanding. There will be those who sharply disagree — some because they feel he is too strict, some because he is not strict enough, and others who figure he has some ulterior motive. Nevertheless, I have chosen to take that risk. Because I have not condemned *all* cases of divorce and *all* people who divorce, some will accuse me of encouraging everyone to rush right down to the courthouse and file for divorce! This is most certainly not my position.

I could here mention various reasons why marriages were dissolved in the Bible such as: neglect (Exodus 21:10, 11), incompatibility (Deut. 21:14), uncleanness (Deut. 24:1), fornication (Matt. 19:9), family problems (Gen. 21:9-12), desertion (1 Cor. 7:15), a husband or wife not being pleased to remain in a marriage (1 Cor. 7:12, 13), mixed marriage (Ezra 10:3), and various causes (Jer. 3:8). With this information before us, I could enlarge on these reasons and produce a list of things that are just as bad or worse — things such as insanity, attempted murder, chronic alcoholism, rebellion, hatred, hypocrisy, dishonesty in business for which the other person could be held financially responsible, constant strife because of religious differences, etc. But a list with more rules is not the answer. Dr. Hudson has written:

> "Are people bettered by having fixed, unalterable rules about divorce and remarriage? Or can they be challenged to set up *ideals,* move toward goals of stability, and commit themselves to being continuously *caring* people? . . . There are *not* in the scriptures, even the whole New Testament, nor in the official statements of all the churches together,

enough instructions to cover *all* the complicated cases that will be seen in actual life."[35]

The Bible gives principles that can serve as guidelines, but one will not find a verse for each specific divorce situation. Each case is different. Every person must be fully persuaded in his own mind concerning the decision to divorce. He must ask if a better purpose can be served by two individuals staying together, or would it be better if the marriage was dissolved. Only the individuals concerned can know the intimate details, the problems, the pros and cons of a marriage. These are deeply involved questions and Christians with conscience will not take them lightly.

Though fornication provides Biblical grounds for divorce, not all details — *even about this* — are explained in the Bible. Certain decisions still have to be made by the individual. Should a woman, for example, divorce a husband who is unfaithful one time? How many times might a man be untrue, or how many women might be involved, before she should file for divorce? What if her nagging, her temper, or her coldness was a partial cause for his marital mistakes? How much guilt rests on her? If a woman does not divorce an unfaithful husband because she thought God never permits divorce, may she do so later if she comes to a different conclusion?

Other questions for which one will not find *specific* answers in the Bible include the following: What if a man's first marriage was in Mexico and not recognized in the United States — can he as an American citizen remarry since his first marriage was not legal? What about a man who lived with a woman for a year with no marriage license — can he later marry someone else? What if a man's wife joins a church that tells her she must go back to her first husband. If she does, who can *he* go back to if he was never married before? What if a girl lived in a foreign country in which her father and the groom's father made the marriage contract — is she forever bound to a contract that someone else made for her?

A PAPER POPE?

If a person had to have an exact "scripture" for every detail of life, people in many, many situations would never have an answer. This does not in any way discredit the truth of the Bible. We simply need to recognize that God never intended the Bible to be a paper pope. It is not merely a book of rules. As we mature in Christ, it becomes apparent that God wants us to do some thinking for ourselves. We should not be afraid to do this, for when we have Christ within, he is the living Word (Col. 1:27; John 1:1). The Christian is not without the spiritual ability to make decisions—even when he may not be able to turn to a specific verse for that decision (cf. 1 Cor. 6:2, 3). Some things we know because the anointing of the Holy Spirit makes them real to us (1 John 2:27).

If a person had to find a verse in the Bible for every detail in life in order to walk with God, such would have been impossible for men like Enoch and Noah. They did not have the Bible; it had not been written yet. Abraham did not have the Bible, yet he was called "the friend of God." Even the early church survived and grew without what we call the New Testament, for it was only then in the process of being written! Even after the 66 books of the Bible were circulated as one book— *many* years later—it was not until after the invention of the printing press that the average person could afford his own copy. Most didn't know how to read anyhow. Nevertheless, through all of these centuries there were people who knew God! Their God was bigger than a book.

There have been people who would not eat potatoes or tomatoes—because they could not find these words in the Bible! As far as that goes, the word "Bible" is not in the Bible either! There are other things—definitely mentioned in the Bible—but an improper interpretation of these things could also lead to some strange conclusions. I must ask a degree of patience on the part of the reader as I give a few examples.

BIBLICAL RULES?

In Eden, Adam and Eve were naked (Gen. 2:25). Would this prove all people should become nudists? When they sinned, God provided clothing made from hides (Gen. 3:21). Would this prove people should wear only leather or furs? Man was to work and sweat (Gen. 3:19). Would this mean people should not use deodorant?

A hand shake would now be considered more appropriate than an ancient custom mentioned in the Bible (Gen. 24:2). Our ideas of hospitality would not require us to turn our daughter out to a lustful mob (Gen. 19:8). David killed at least one hundred Philistine men, bringing back their foreskins as a bride price (1 Sam. 18:25). Surely most would find a diamond ring more appropriate!

I doubt if any church would recommend for an elderly pastor the method used to warm up David when he was old and cold (1 Kings 1:1, 2). King Solomon had one thousand women in his harem (1 Kings 11:3), but this provides no example to be followed today. It did not work out very well then!

Hosea married a prostitute (Hosea 1:2). Would this prove preachers should marry prostitutes? Once the Benjamites, with no romance or courting, chose wives simply on the basis of the physical features they observed while the girls danced (Judges 21:21). Esther was chosen as queen because she was one of the finalists in a beauty contest — each of which spent a night with the king and from which he made his choice. Prior to this each girl was bathed and perfumed for one year (Esther 2:12-14). Would any advise such practices for a young girl in the church today? Moses recommended a one year honeymoon for newlyweds — for one year the man was to do no business, just stay home and cheer up his wife! (Deut. 24:5).

Everyone recognizes that these and many more customs, ideas, and concepts — though mentioned in the Bible — were not ntended as the basis for inflexible rules for twentieth century Christians. *It is apparent that the proper context and setting for verses must be carefully considered.*

All of this is so true in what we have seen about divorce and remarriage. Those who take the statement of Jesus that was aimed, primarily, against a certain divorce custom of that time — divorce "for every cause" — and try to apply it to all types of divorce today and to all cases of divorce, have surely misapplied scripture. They have built a doctrinal monstrosity out of the idea that God *never* permits divorce. They condemn all cases of divorce and remarriage as adultery, and then tend to limit God's forgiveness and grace to those who break up their marriages and live in celibacy.

Even though Jesus said — in the same passage — that the single life was *not* intended for "*all* men," those who teach the celibacy doctrine require it for all men who have been through a divorce! They must teach, contrary to Genesis 2:18, that it *is* good for a man to be alone — if he had a previous marriage! They overlook the fact that Paul granted the right of marriage to "*every* man" and "*every* woman" — including, obviously, those who have had a previous marriage. They fail to realize that their practice of "*forbidding* to marry," is a doctrine that is condemned in the New Testament and not even thought of in the Old.

Marriage was made for man, and not man for marriage (cf. Mark 2:27). That is, God did not make marriage and then make a man and a woman just so someone could get married! No, he created a man and a woman and instituted marriage for them. It was intended for their happiness and peace; it was designed to be a blessing and benefit. This — not divorce — was the original ideal. But when a marriage degenerates into a state in which neither party is benefited or blessed, if being tied to another person becomes marital martyrdom, if it becomes hurtful and disastrous, divorce, as a last resort, is a *Biblically recognized alternative.* To say the Bible condemns all cases of divorce—"all the way from Genesis to Revelation"—is simply *not* true. This book, by the grace of God, may be destined to help correct this misconception and heal some of the hurt this misconception has caused.

NOTES

1. *The Interpreter's Bible* (Nashville: Abingdon-Cokesbury Press), Vol. 2, p. 473.
2. *Ibid,* Vol. 6, p. 1136.
3. *Clarke's Commentary* (Nashville: Abingdon Press), Vol. 6, p. 228.
4. Flavius Josephus, *Antiquities of the Jews* (Philadelphia: The John C. Winston Company, 1957 edition), Book 4, 8:23.
5. Guy Duty, *Divorce and Remarriage* (Minneapolis: Bethany Fellowship, 1967), pp. 21, 22. See also the commentaries, Jewish encyclopedias, etc.
6. Charles B. Williams, *The New Testament — A Private Translation in the Language of the People* (Chicago: Moody Press, 1956), p. 173, note on Luke 16:18.
7. A. Edersheim, *The Life and Times of Jesus the Messiah* (New York: Longmans, Green, 1897), Vol. 2, p. 332.
8. R. Lofton Hudson, *'Til Divorce Do Us Part* (Nashville: Thomas Nelson, 1973), p. 49.
9. Jay E. Adams, *Marriage, Divorce, and Remarriage* (Grand Rapids: Baker Book House, 1980), p. 38.
10. *Encyclopedia of Religion and Ethics,* James Hastings, editor (New York: Charles Scribner Sons, 1928), Vol. 1, p. 132.
11. Richard Francis Weymouth, *The New Testament in Modern Speech* (New York: Harper and Brothers, 1929), p. 12.
12. John Calvin, *Harmony of the Evangelists* (Grand Rapids: Eerdmans Publishing Company), pp. 383, 384.
13. *Pulpit Commentary* (New York: Funk and Wagnalls), Vol. 36, p. 67.
14. George M. Lamsa, *The Holy Bible from Ancient Eastern Manuscripts* (Philadelphia: A. J. Holman Company, 1961), p. 955.
15. Hudson, *'Till Divorce Do Us Part,* p. 48.
16. Ralph Woodrow, *Babylon Mystery Religion — Ancient and Modern* (Riverside, California: Ralph Woodrow Evangelistic Association, 1966).
17. B. L. Woolf, *Reformation Writings of Martin Luther* (London: Lutterworth Press, 1952), p. 307. Quoted by Duty, p. 118.
18. Bob W. Brown, *Getting Married Again* (Waco, Texas: Word Books, 1979), p. 15.
19. Williams, *The New Testament — A Private Translation in the Language of the People,* p. 371.
20. M. R. Vincent, *Word Studies in the New Testament* (Grand Rapids: Eerdmans Company, 1957), Vol. 3, p. 219.
21. Duty, *Marriage and Divorce,* pp. 110, 111.
22. Finis Jennings Dake, *Dake's Annotated Reference Bible* (Atlanta: Dake Bible Sales, 1965), p. 180.

23. *Clarke's Commentary,* Vol. 6, p. 223.
24. B. L. Woolf, *Reformation Writings of Martin Luther,* p. 307.
25. *Clarke's Commentary,* Vol. 6, p. 610.
26. *Twentieth Century Encyclopedia of Religious Knowledge* (Grand Rapids: Baker Book House, 1955), p. 344.
27. Hudson, *'Til Divorce Do Us Part,* p. 25.
28. *Ibid.,* the case of Jerry and Ann, pp. 86-88, quoted by permission.
29. Jimmy Swaggart, "Divorce and Subsequent Marriage," in *The Evangelist* magazine, Sept. 1979 (Baton Rouge: Jimmy Swaggart Evangelistic Association), p. 5.
30. *Ibid.,* p. 4.
31. Ibid., p. 5.
32. Brown, *Getting Married Again,* pp. 28, 29.
33. William Barclay, *Ethics in a Permissive Society* (London: Collins, Fontana Books, 1971), pp. 203, 204. Quoted by Hudson, p. 81.
34. Geoffrey F. Fisher, *Problems of Marriage and Divorce* (New York: Morehouse-Gorham Company, 1955), p. 21.
35. Hudson, *'Til Divorce Do Us Part,* pp. 50, 51.